D-DAY
BOMBER COMMAND
FAILED TO RETURN

Published in 2014 by Fighting High Ltd
www.fightinghigh.com

British Library Cataloguing-in-Publication data. A CIP record
for this title is available from the British Library.

ISBN 978 0 9926207 1 4

Designed by Michael Lindley www.truthstudio.co.uk.
Printed and bound in China by Toppan Leefung Printing Limited

D-DAY

FAILED TO RETURN

BOMBER COMMAND

STEVE DARLOW, SEAN FEAST, MARC HALL, ANDREW MACDONALD
HOWARD SANDALL AND PETER COOK

FH

CONTENTS

68

30

10

44

110

78

54

36

98

22

86

FOREWORD

BY WING COMMANDER JOHN BELL, MBE, DFC

(RAF BOMBER COMMAND BOMB AIMER, NOS 619 AND 617 SQUADRONS)

Above John Bell, 2012. *Tim Humphries, Astonleigh Studio*

Opposite page John Bell, second from right, with his crew in December 1943; John's logbook recording his D-Day operation.

ON NEW YEAR'S DAY 1944, Great Britain and her Allies entered the fifth year of war with Nazi Germany. Bomber Command's Battle of Berlin was at its height as the Royal Air Force crews fought their way across 600 miles of hostile territory to bomb the capital of the German government. On the evening of that day, my crew and I took off to join a force of 420 Lancasters. It was my eighth trip to Berlin, which had the heaviest defences of all German cities, and the reception this night was no different – a dark sky filled with shell bursts and with night fighters patrolling the approaches. It seemed impossible to get through the mass of exploding shells but somehow we made it unscathed. Not so the unfortunate crews of the two bombers we saw plunging earthwards in flames – a sight that made us very much aware of the fine line between a lucky escape and total disaster. We returned to our base after eight hours of flying to eventually hear that twenty-eight Lancasters, 196 aircrew were missing.

A few months later, on the night of 5/6 June, I was in a No. 617 Squadron Lancaster carrying out a quite different operation, *Taxable*, a non-bombing 'raid' on the French coast near Le Havre to divert the attention of the German forces from the invasion fleets approaching the Normandy beaches. It was a deception of great importance to the success of the initial D-Day landings and I remember the enthusiastic reaction of the whole squadron in respect of their involvement in this historic event.

Bomber Command crews continued to play a vital role in support of the invasion forces as they established a firm base in France and continued the advance into Germany. This was not without suffering considerable losses to the Luftwaffe pilots, who continued to provide determined resistance to the end of hostilities. The immense courage, unimaginable hardships, and sacrifice of the Bomber Command crews supporting the invasion is told in great detail in this well-researched volume. The stories of those who did not return to their homeland bring to life the deeds of the bomber crews. It is a tribute to all the airmen who died in the service of their country and the defence of freedom – airmen who are now depicted and commemorated by the seven bronze figures of the Bomber Command Memorial, unveiled in London's Green Park on 28 June 2012.

O N 6 JUNE 1944 THE ALLIES LAUNCHED ONE OF THE GREATEST MILITARY FEATS OF ALL TIME, FORCING A RE-ENTRY INTO 'FORTRESS EUROPE' – THE SEABORNE AND AIRBORNE ASSAULT UPON THE COASTLINE OF NORMANDY. KEY TO THE SUCCESS OF THE D-DAY CAMPAIGN WAS THE CONTRIBUTION OF THE ROYAL AIR FORCE'S BOMBER COMMAND, WHO WAGED AN UNRELENTING CAMPAIGN IN THE RUN-UP TO D-DAY, ON THE DAY ITSELF, AND IN THE MONTHS SUBSEQUENT. BOMBER COMMAND AIRCREW ATTACKED RAILYARDS AND COMMUNICATIONS TARGETS TO ISOLATE THE BATTLE AREA FROM ENEMY REINFORCEMENT, BOMBARDED ENEMY POSITIONS, SUPPLIED THE FRENCH RESISTANCE AND DECEIVED THE ENEMY AS TO THE TRUE WHEREABOUTS OF THE BEACH LANDINGS.

THE COST IN YOUNG LIVES WAS, HOWEVER, ENORMOUS. THOUSANDS OF YOUNG BOMBER COMMAND

AIRCREW SACRIFICED THEIR LIVES ATTACKING INVASION TARGETS IN THE THREE MONTHS PRIOR TO THE BEACH LANDINGS. MORE AIRMEN FAILED TO RETURN ON D-DAY ITSELF. NUMEROUS OTHERS NOW EITHER REST IN FRENCH OR BELGIAN CEMETERIES OR ARE LISTED AS MISSING AS A RESULT OF FURTHER RAIDS IN SUPPORT OF THE NORMANDY LAND CAMPAIGN. ON 1 JULY 1944 COMMANDER-IN-CHIEF OF BOMBER COMMAND, AIR CHIEF MARSHAL SIR ARTHUR HARRIS, WROTE TO CHIEF OF AIR STAFF SIR CHARLES PORTAL EXPRESSING HIS CONCERN OVER THE LACK OF RECOGNITION IN RESPECT OF HIS COMMAND'S SUPPORT OF THE INVASION. 'THERE ARE 10,500 AIRCREW IN MY OPERATIONAL SQUADRONS. IN THREE MONTHS WE HAVE LOST OVER HALF THAT NUMBER. THEY HAVE A RIGHT THAT THEIR STORY SHOULD BE ADEQUATELY TOLD, AND IT IS A MILITARY NECESSITY THAT IT SHOULD BE.'

"NO ENEMY PLANE WILL FLY OVER THE REICH TERRITORY"
HERMAN GOERING

Men of No. 467 Squadron, Royal Australian Air Force, celebrate the completion of 100 operations by the Avro Lancaster R5868 'PO-S' (S for Sugar) after its sortie on 11/12 May 1944 to a pre-invasion communications target in Belgium. *Imperial War Museum*

CHAPTER ONE

ALWAYS REMEMBERED

BY STEVE DARLOW

IT WAS THE VIEW OF THE COMMANDER OF BOMBER COMMAND, AIR CHIEF MARSHAL SIR ARTHUR HARRIS, THAT THERE WAS A CONSIDERABLE LESSENING OF RISK TO HIS BOMBER CREWS WHEN THEY WERE ATTACKING TARGETS IN OCCUPIED FRANCE AND BELGIUM. IN THE MONTHS PRIOR TO BOMBER COMMAND IMPLEMENTING ITS FULL COMMITMENT TO OPERATION OVERLORD, THE ATTRITION RATES HAD BEEN HIGH, EXCESSIVELY SO, PERHAPS EVEN UNSUSTAINABLE HAD HARRIS CONTINUED WITH HIS DIRECT ASSAULT UPON GERMANY. BUT AGAINST THE ODDS MANY BOMBER COMMAND AIRMEN WOULD SURVIVE THE FIERCE AIR BATTLES OF THE EARLY MONTHS OF 1944, AND THEN TAKE PART IN THE PERCEIVED 'EASIER' RAIDS SUPPORTING THE INVASION. NAVIGATOR JOHN (JACK) LOTT WAS ONE SUCH AIRMAN, COMING THROUGH EACH COMBAT, INCLUDING A CRASH, ONLY TO LOSE HIS LIFE, AS HIS TOUR WAS ABOUT TO END, DIRECTLY SUPPORTING THE BATTLE FOR THE D-DAY BEACHHEADS.

JOHN ERNEST LOTT was born in Chiswick on 25 May 1919 and as his service record states, 'enlisted for the emergency' a few months short of his twenty-first birthday. Jack passed through No. 1 School of Air Navigation in Canada, and No. 31 Air Navigation School, arriving back in the UK early in October 1942. Passing through No. 11 Operational Training Unit at RAF Westcott and No. 1657 Conversion Unit at RAF Stradishall, Jack arrived at No. 75 New Zealand Squadron on 18 April 1943.

In May 1943 Jack returned to No. 11 OTU and the following month left the UK for the Middle East Pool. However, his service record shows him returning to 'Home Establishment' in August, although it is unclear why. Two months at No. 29 OTU was followed by familiarisation with a four-engined heavy bomber at No. 1661 Conversion Unit, RAF Winthorpe, with further experience gained at No. 5 Lancaster Finishing School in December. On 8 January 1944 Jack arrived at No. 619 Squadron in the midst of playing their part in Bomber Command's assault on the German 'Big City', the 'Battle of Berlin'.

Jack was described by his flight engineer Jack Forrest as having a sardonic sense of humour and a prodigious memory. On occasions when the

Left and inset Jack Lott at No. 31 ANS Port Albert, Canada. *Roger Olden*

crew went to the pub Jack would ask them all to name an object. Following a 'skinful' in the pub Jack would then recite what was said and who had said it. Jack was also noted for his inquisitive mind, but such curiosity appears to have been held at bay when on operations. He was certainly not prone to venture from behind his navigator's curtain while on a bombing raid. On one occasion, when the flak was particularly bad, Jack had been summoned to stand next to his pilot in the cockpit. When he saw what was going on outside, a 'sod this' followed, and for the rest of the tour Jack remained cocooned with his maps and navigational aids.

Jack's navigational skills first directed his Australian skipper, Kim Roberts, to Magdeburg on the night of 21/22 January 1944, the attacking bomber force suffering high casualties, with 57 aircraft lost. And the high attrition rates continued on their next three raids, all to Berlin: 28/29 January (46 aircraft lost); 30/31 January (33 aircraft); and 15/16 February (43 aircraft). On the last raid of January the crew's teamwork had prevented their plane becoming one of these dismal statistics. Sergeant Johnny Tucker, the wireless operator, had picked up an aircraft on the 'Visual Monica' tail warning radar at 1,000 yards and when the rear gunner, Sergeant Lionel Virgo (RAAF), saw a Junkers 88 at 800 yards he barked the order to corkscrew to Kim Roberts and then opened fire, joined by his colleague Sergeant Johnny Williams in the mid-upper

Left Jack Lott at Kincardine on Lake Huron. *Roger Olden*

WILL YE NO
COME
BACK AGAIN

Right Jack Lott.
Roger Olden

turret. It appeared their enemy did not return fire and was lost to sight.

On their next raid to Berlin it was not enemy action that led to a casualty among the crew. Even if Bomber Command airmen did return from a raid to Germany unscathed, they still had to land their aircraft in wartime conditions, at night, and weather could be the new enemy. On this occasion Kim Roberts had piloted a Lancaster borrowed from No. 630 Squadron, to which it would not be returning. On the approach to land, a combination of poor visibility and another aircraft's slow landing resulted in an overshoot, the Lancaster circuiting at 700 feet. As the four-engined bomber came into the landing funnel it struck the ground. Jack Forrest recalls: 'I don't remember anything else until I woke up in the wreckage of the Lancaster with the trunk of a tree an inch or two away from my face. … Berlin had been more welcoming.' The rear gunner suffered severe injuries, the rest of the crew minor wounds, and the aircraft was written off.

Just over a week later the crew were back on operations, sent to Schweinfurt, with a new rear gunner who was called into action as they flew to the target. The wireless operator had alerted the crew to a contact 1,500 yards astern, which became an order for Kim Roberts to throw the Lancaster into a corkscrew once the Ju88 had closed to 800 yards. The rear gunner unleashed his guns as the enemy aircraft sped across below him at 300 yards range. Contact was lost.

Raids to Augsburg and Stuttgart followed, and on the night of 10/11 March they bombed the aircraft factory at Châteauroux, France, their squadron diary entry recording that they 'orbited 6 times after bombing. After leaving target bombs seen to explode beneath the roof of buildings.' On 15/16 March it was back to Germany, part of an 863 aircraft raid on Stuttgart. Once more the air gunners would be called into action.

In recognition of his skill that night Kim Roberts would be awarded an immediate DFC and rear gunner Gill King a DFM.

For Jack Lott and his crew there would be no letup. Two trips to Frankfurt followed, bombing from 20,000 feet and 21,000 feet respectively, along with a raid on Essen, bombing from 19,300 feet, prior to the crew being detailed for the historic attack on Nurem-

```
Combat report
for J/619 Squadron, 15/16 March 1944

Pilot: Pilot Officer Roberts
Navigator: Flight Sergeant Lott
Flight Engineer: Sergeant Forrest
Air Bomber: Sergeant De Viell
Wireless Operator: Sergeant Tucker
Mid Upper Gunner: Sergeant Williams
Rear Gunner: Flight Sergeant King

Target - Stuttgart


On the night of 15/16 March 1944,
Lancaster Mk. III 'J' of No. 619
Squadron over target area at 23.23
hrs, height 20,000 ft, heading 004
IAS 160 visibility good in starlight,
9/10ths cloud below at 12,000 ft.
W/Operator contacted aircraft
1200-1500 yards starboard quarter up.
Rear gunner saw Ju.88 visually at
800 yds. still starboard quarter up.
Rear Gunner gave order to corkscrew
starboard. E/A opened fire at 800
yds. but failed to connect. Rear
Gunner opened up at approx. 700 yds.
E/A broke away at approx. 400 yds.
port quarter down. Captain resumed
course, rear gunner then gave
corkscrew port as E/A returned to
attack from port quarter up range
600 yds and scored hits on Lancaster
'J'. Rear and M.U. gunners opened
fire but after short burst all six
guns failed to operate owing to No. 2
stoppages in both starboards and No.
1 stoppages in both port guns. Mid
Upper guns failed with both No. 2
stoppages. The corkscrew was
continued for 8¼ minutes during which
the E/A fired a further 4 bursts. A/G
had by this time cleared port outer
gun and opened fire at 50-75 yds.
range, the E/A's port engine burst
into flames and Ju.88 was last seen
by Flight engineer and Mid Upper in
vertical dive into cloud.
    During these attacks Lanc 'J' was
hit by cannon fire, port rudder being
shot away, also port side of A/C was
raked with cannon shell shrapnel. E/A
claimed destroyed.


Rear Gunner fired off 150 rounds per
gun.
M/U Gunner fired off 100 rounds per
gun.
```

berg on the night of 30/31 March 1944, which proved to be Bomber Command's worst night of the entire war. Kim Roberts brought his crew home safely that night, but ninety-five of his pilot colleagues, and their crews, were not so fortunate.

The crew's initial raid in April 1944, was also their first one directly in support of the pre-invasion bombing directives. At 0133 hours on the night of 10/11 April, Sergeant de Viell released the bombs from 6,250 feet on the rail yards at Tours, the low level reflecting the emphasis on accuracy when attacking targets in 'friendly' territory. The next night the explosives dropped by Sergeant de Viell contributed to a devastating attack on Aachen, and a week later the rail yards at Juvisy passed through his bombsight. It was back to Germany for the following three raids – to Brunswick, Munich and Schweinfurt – followed by an attack on an airframe factory at Oslo on 28/29 April.

At this stage of the war a main-force Bomber Command aircrew was expected to complete thirty operations in their tour of duty, although in the first months of 1944 the odds were definitely against any crews reaching such a number. A simple statistical analysis of the operations flown by Jack Lott provides a suitable example. In respect of operations to German targets up until the end of April, Jack flew over hostile territory sixteen times. In total Bomber Command lost 476 aircraft on these raids – a loss rate of 4.9%. Jack had survived odds that were slightly worse than one in two – and he was only midway through his tour. During this period Jack had also completed three raids to French targets, on which

Bomber Command lost two aircraft – a loss rate of just under 0.5%.

Such operational statistics were not lost on the RAF's heavy bomber commanders. Air Vice-Marshal Don Bennett, commander of the Pathfinder Force, subsequently wrote in his book *Pathfinder* that when it came to operations directly supporting the invasion, the crews had 'a relative holiday from the intense receptions to which they were accustomed in Germany'.

Sir Arthur Harris had quickly picked up on what he believed. In a dispatch of 8 March 1944 he made it clear that he viewed the 'risk, fatigue and strain' of operations such as those against French targets as being, 'in no way comparable' to raids on German targets and that some aircrews would undergo far less risk than others, 'which is obviously undesirable'. With the forthcoming escalation in the number of raids to these easier targets he was also concerned that crews would finish their tours too quickly, which could compromise the strength of the operational squadrons. As such he instigated a policy of certain raids only counting as one-third of an operation against a tour of duty. Such a policy, while understandable, was not in general met favourably by the crews.

Into May and the emphasis on Bomber Command's targeting priorities virtually became exclusive to strategic invasion targets. Seven raids featured in Jack Lott's logbook for the month: the aircraft assembly factory at Toulouse (1/2 May), the German Army

Left Jack's identity
card – form 1250.
Roger Olden

camp at Mailly-le-Camp (3/4 May), an ammunition dump at Salbris (7/8 May), the Gnome and Rhône factory at Gennevilliers (9/10 May), the military camp at Bourg-Leopold (11/12 May), the rail yards at Amiens (19/20 May) and then back to Germany and Brunswick (22/23 May).

In the first few days of June 1944, as the day of invasion approached, the Bomber Command targeting became more tactical in nature. At the conclusion of the Allied Air Commanders' conference on 3 June the task for the RAF heavies was made clear. The aircrews were to attack beach defences and blast and block the road and rail networks through which the Germans would be sending reinforcements – thereby supporting the establishment of footholds on the Normandy beaches codenamed Gold, Juno, Sword, Omaha and Utah, and ensuring the Allies won the battle of the build-up as the beachheads were ex-

panded. In addition Bomber Command would be carrying out various diversion ruses to confuse the Germans as to the true whereabouts of the landings.

On 5 June 1944 over 8,000 Bomber Command airmen prepared to take off on D-Day operations. A total of 1,012 Lancaster, Halifaxes and Mosquitoes took off to bomb ten coastal gun batteries that defended the sea approaches to the Normandy beaches, one of which was the No.619 Squadron Lancaster flown by Flight Lieutenant Roberts, detailed to try and take out the guns at La Pernelle. The No.619 Squadron diarist's account of the operation is a fine piece of understatement considering the historic event the crews had just taken part in: 'D-DAY. All aircraft returned safely from the previous night's operation, reporting that they had observed tremendous activity across the Channel. This was the start of the attack on Western Europe. Orders were ordered for the night. Crews carried out ground runs during the

Right Jack Lott, second row up, sixth from the right. The unit is unknown but believed to be during training in the UK. *Roger Olden*

Right Kim Roberts.
Roger Olden

afternoon.' In respect of the results of the strikes on the gun batteries, subsequent analysis initially suggested success although weather conditions may have hampered accuracy. Indeed it had, with limited damage, but enemy prisoners would later report that the attacks had adversely affected morale.

The atmosphere was optimistic at the late morning Allied Air Commanders' conference on 6 June. Beachheads had been established, but had yet to be linked. A close eye was kept on enemy troop movements, with a rapid response required. It is testament to the efficiency and dedication of all those involved in the operations of Bomber Command that later that night 1,065 aircraft took off to attack enemy lines of communication. The diarist of No. 619 Squadron would record: 'All aircraft took off to attack a road and rail bridge at Caen where our Paratroops were attempting to hold up attempts to attack the Beachhead.' Kim Roberts's Lancaster took off from RAF Dunholme Lodge at 0055 hours on 7 June 1944. For the action the crew had a new member in the rear turret. The raid of the night before had been the last of Gill King's tour and he was replaced by Guy Wyand, who was beginning a second tour.

Right Short Stirling at No. 1657 Conversion Unit, RAF Stradishall, where Jack first familiarised himself with a four-engined bomber.
Roger Olden

Charges to pay

POST OFFICE

No. _____

OFFICE STAMP

RECEI 54 W 4 916644 7 TH 1944 LI/T

Prefix. Time handed in. Office of Origin and Service Instructions. Words.

76

From _____ m 76 11:30 LI/T OHMS RTY CO 63⅜ m

PRIORITY CC MRS E OLDEN 54 UPHAMPARK ROAD

LONDON W 4 =

DEEPLY REGRET TO INFORM YOU YOUR BROTHER 916644
W/O JOHN ERNEST LOTT IS MISSING FROM AIR
OPERATIONS 7 TH JUNE 1944 LETTER FOLLOWS AND
FURTHER INFORMATION RECEIVED WILL BE
FORWARDED TO YOU IMMEDIATELY PENDING RECEIPT OF
WRITTEN CONFIRMATIONS FROM THE AIR MINSITRY NO
INFORMATIONS SHOULD BE GIVEN TO THE PRESS =
OC 609 SQUADRON DUNHOLME LODGE +

Left The missing telegram (with incorrect squadron number). *Roger Olden*

Left Guy Wyand.
Via the Wyand family

Having bombed the target Kim Roberts set course for home, heading for the Cherbourg peninsula and flying at less than 2,000 feet, beneath the cloud. Soon John Tucker became suspicious of a reading on the electronic device, Fishpond, suggesting an enemy fighter approaching their Lancaster, although neither gunner was able to see anything. Tucker remained worried and his fears were soon realised. Jack Forrest would later record: 'Within seconds there was a tremendous bang and crash, the aircraft shuddered, Kim took immediate evasive action, started to corkscrew, and I heard a scream from the rear gunner as we were attacked again by the Ju88. I saw a stream of tracer rush past and hit both starboard engines, which immediately caught fire.' The pilot tried to contact his crew but heard nothing from his wireless operator or gunners. Then, as Jack Forrest recalls, 'the fighter came in again, guns and cannons blazing, and the inner port engine caught fire'. Kim Roberts ordered: 'Abandon aircraft chaps.' Jack Forrest records: 'The pilot's chute was passed over and clipped on and there was time only to glimpse the flames streaking back forty feet from three Merlin engines and Kim struggling to keep the bomber level.' Reg de Viell exited the escape hatch, followed by Jack Forrest, 'We were no higher than 1,700 feet when I went out', and they would be the only men to survive. After a few days' evasion both Jack and Reg were captured and saw out the war as prisoners. It was not until they returned that they learned the fate of their crewmates, the aircraft coming to ground in a field at Baupte, near Auvers. Over the years further information came to light. A young boy had watched Kim Roberts struggling to control and land the burning Lancaster, and then witnessed flames engulfing the pilot, who was still in the crashed Lancaster cockpit. No remains were ever found. Reports came through that two men had bailed out but had not survived. The bodies of the four men found were originally buried at Auvers.

On 7 June 1944 a telegram was sent to Mrs Sylvia Olden: 'Deeply regret to inform you your brother 916644 W/O John Ernest Lott is missing from Air Operations …' and an optimistic letter from Jack's squadron soon followed with further information.

He was Navigator on an aircraft detailed to attack Caen, in Normandy. As is usual, silence was maintained after take-off and, therefore, it is not possible to determine at the moment the cause of its failure to return. Your brother was a member of a very experienced crew and I am sure that the Pilot, Flight Lieutenant K. Roberts, would do everything possible to ensure their safety. There is, of course, every possibility that they abandoned the aircraft and landed safely in enemy occupied territory and, if this is the case, news should reach you from the Air Ministry within the next few weeks. We can only hope that they are safe and that you will be hearing shortly.

But subsequent correspondence confirmed that 25-year-old Jack Lott had been killed on a bombing operation in direct support of the Normandy landings. He is now buried at the Bayeux War Cemetery, one of the cemetery's 4,144 Commonwealth burials of the Second World War, his gravestone displaying 'Always remembered by his sisters Sylvia and Ethel'. 'Johnny' Williams and Guy Wyand are also buried at Bayeux and John Tucker is interred at Tilly-sur-Seulles War Cemetery, one of 990 Commonwealth Second World War burials. Kim Roberts is named on the Air Forces Memorial at Runnymede, which commemorates those with no known grave. ●

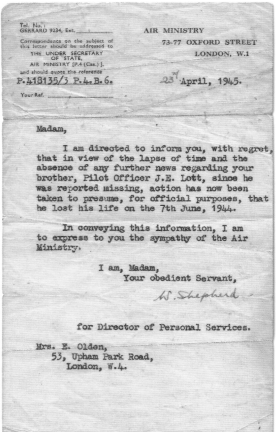

Opposite The memorial to Kim Roberts and the crew of Lancaster LL783, Auvers, 6 June 1996. Front row from left to right; Jack Forrest, Reg de Viell, Ian Roberts (Kim Roberts nephew) Newton Roberts (Kim Roberts younger brother) and Gil King. Back row from left to right; Kim Roberts (Kim Roberts nephew), The Australian Air Attaché and Ivor 'Chopper' Powell (Flight Engineer 619 Squadron). *Via Forrest family*

From left Reg de Viell at John Williams's grave in 1996, Bayeux War Cemetery; Jack Forrest; Jack Forrest at Guy Wyand's grave in 1996, Bayeux War Cemetery. *Via Forrest family*

CHAPTER TWO

ELEVEN DAYS IN MAY

BY ANDREW MACDONALD

FRED AND JOY BUNNAGAR ENDED EACH DAY IN QUIET CONTEMPLATION. AFTER RETIRING TO BED, THE TWO DEEPLY DEVOUT CHRISTIANS WOULD KNEEL TOGETHER AT THE FOOT OF THEIR BED AND PRAY FOR THEIR THREE YOUNG SONS. THE TWO ELDEST WERE ALREADY IN UNIFORM AND THE THIRD, MERCIFULLY, WAS FAR TOO YOUNG FOR MILITARY SERVICE AND JOY HOPED IT WOULD REMAIN THAT WAY. WITH GOD'S GRACE THEIR THOUGHTS AND PRAYERS WOULD BE ANSWERED, AND WITH THEIR MINDS MOMENTARILY AT EASE, THE TWO COULD QUIETLY DRIFT OFF TO SLEEP. BUT ONE NIGHT IN PARTICULAR, ON 12 MAY 1944, JOY'S MIND WAS TURNING OVER CONTINUOUSLY AND SHE COULD NOT SLEEP AT ALL WELL. SHE ROSE IN SOME DISTRESS, TURNED TO HER HUSBAND AND WHISPERED INTO HIS EAR. SHE KNEW, AS ONLY A MOTHER COULD, THAT SOMETHING WAS DESPERATELY WRONG AND THAT ONE SON, MAURICE, WAS IN GRAVE DANGER.

PERHAPS IT WAS a mother's intuition that alerted her, or every bit as likely her unshakeable faith in her Lord God. Whatever it may have been, the timing could not have been more ominous. The two were now wide awake and they slipped out of bed to pray earnestly for their gallant young son. It was in God's hands now and all they could do was hope, pray and wait for news that their son was safe and well. At that very moment, several hundred miles away from their quiet suburban house, a Lancaster bomber had ceased to exist, taking with her all seven young airmen in the blink of an eye. The captain was Pilot Officer Maurice Bunnagar from Merseyside in Liverpool. He was only twenty years old.

Maurice was born at the family home in Tuebrook, Liverpool, in September 1923. He was the second of three boys. Alan arrived first in 1920 and Ralph much later on in 1929. They all went to Lister Drive Council School and also attended one of two Sunday schools. They were raised on strong moral values and while Joy nurtured her children, Fred maintained the discipline in the household. He had high expectations of all his boys and did not suffer fools gladly. They were all bright and accomplished children. Alan became a draftsman before the war, and when Maurice had completed secondary school he obtained an apprenticeship with the great toymaker, Meccano, and worked as a toolmaker until the outbreak of the Second World War. This was the perfect job for him as he was absolutely mad about aircraft. He made the dyes for the Hawker Hurricane, the aircraft that would forever be remembered as the saviour of the Battle of Britain. After war was declared Meccano turned its giant resources over to the war effort. Maurice's skills were more than enough to preclude him from entering service but he grew weary of watching his childhood mates disappear into the armed services, and with his sights firmly set on realising a childhood dream, he pestered his father Fred to release him into the care of the Royal Air Force. Maurice was barely eighteen years old when he enlisted at Padgate in Manchester. A new adventure awaited him and he was desperate to grab it tightly with his two young hands.

The initial aspects of basic training were undertaken in England. Maurice's first experiences of flying occurred in the Tiger Moth at an Elementary Flying Training School, where he would be quickly assessed to see if the aspiring pilot had the basic aptitude to fly. Maurice soon went solo and was considered sufficiently promising to move to the next stage. He eventually found himself on a ship bound for North America. The Empire Air Training Scheme was one of the great success stories of the Second World War and had been created to train the masses of young aircrew destined for combat. Great Britain used her close ties with her Commonwealth neighbours and allies to send tens of thousands of young men from across the globe to much safer skies and pleasant weather. There were airfields in South Africa, Canada, the USA, even Rhodesia. Maurice was sent to one of the airfields in sunny Florida, probably Clewiston, and he would have resumed his flying instruction alongside fellow American trainees. They were to all intents and purposes American recruits and the only things that distinguished them from the natives were their caps and of course their broad English accents.

Left Maurice Bunnagar.
Ralph Bunnagar

ities were waiting for them when they returned and the ringleader was summarily stripped of his wings – just long enough for the punishment to sink in, as the wings were soon returned. After all, they needed good pilots with initiative!

By 1943 most if not all of these young men had returned to England to complete the final stages of their flying training and progress to operational stations. The RAF increasingly found itself in need of new aircrew, none more so than Bomber Command where the loss rates were becoming unacceptably high. Accordingly the vast majority of these men were earmarked for bombers, whether it was a lifelong ambition or not. It was still flying after all. Maurice too was destined for Bomber Command and by August 1943 he was sent to No. 16 Operational Training Unit based out of RAF Upper Heyford in Oxfordshire. The airfield, still without concrete runways, operated the sturdy and dependable Wellington bombers and Maurice spent the next three months undertaking the standard exercises required to complete this aspect of his flying career.

The young scouser had no problems converting to Stearmans, Harvards or any other single-engined aircraft he encountered. He was a natural pilot. He made it to the passing-out parade, graduated and proudly received his wings. However, while the Americans were granted two weeks' leave to celebrate with friends and family, the British and Commonwealth boys were told to remain where they were. The last thing the American authorities wanted was a hoard of foreign aircrew wandering around with no particular place to go. It smacked of trouble. They didn't anticipate any objections from the boys on base. Two weeks wasn't long. But they also didn't expect a mass walkout as the boys hotfooted it to Miami in search of fun. Needless to say, the author-

All aircrew of the day would no doubt have identical entries in their logbooks of circuits and landings, cross-country and high-level bombing exercises. It was all part of the training and was drummed into crews until they could do it in their sleep. On one particular mid-winter flight, as they approached the last few days of their instruction, the crew had diverted to a satellite airfield with much shorter runways. As they took off to return home, their wireless set packed up and a decision was made to turn back to the aerodrome they had just left. As Maurice lined the aircraft up for an approach, the flaps also decided that the outside air temperature was much too cold to operate in and they froze solidly. So with no flaps and no radio on a short approach, the Wellington shot down the runway at a rapid rate of knots, past the threshold, through the perimeter fence, and finally came to a standstill in a ploughed field. As the boys scrambled clear of the wreckage, the navigator in a panic set off the self-destruct mechanisms on some of the more sensitive pieces of equipment and consequently left a large hole on an already sorry-looking Wellington. Thankfully no one was hurt and a spell in the local sickbay provided the boys with a moment or two to laugh at their misfortune. There would be precious few opportunities again.

While the pilot was generally acknowledged as the captain of the crew, all of the men relied heavily on one another for mutual support and strong leadership. The bomb aimer and the eldest member was 26-year-old Flying Officer John Isfan from the flat plains of Saskatchewan in Canada. His parents, Tudor and Anna, had both emigrated from Romania and had worked like Trojans to build a sustainable farm out of a hostile landscape, and educate ten children as well. The youngest son Nick is still to this day in awe of his parents' achievements despite their many obstacles. Such hardships of course only helped to make their children more dependable and resilient. John was both of these things and much more besides. His rank, age and life experiences made him the ideal father figure for a group of young men who had not long left secondary school.

Arthur Ian Henderson, aged nineteen, came from Crosby in Liverpool, just a few miles from Maurice's family home in Merseyside. Ron Watson, also nineteen, was from Dagenham in Essex. He was the archetypal air gunner: tough, reliable, cheeky and good looking. Having worked in an armaments factory, Ron was exempt from serving and yet he was perfectly prepared to risk his life if it came to that, a very gallant young man. The wireless operator remains a mystery, sadly. His name was John Albert Chambers and he probably came from Preston in Lancashire. John was a tall man of slim build and probably in his late twenties when he joined the crew. Last but not least was the crew's mid-upper gunner, Bernie Easterlow, who had in fact earlier trained as a navigator but evidently remustered at a later stage, though it is not known why. Bernie was born in Foleshill, Coventry, and more than any man knew what it was like to watch a city close to his heart burn. Quite naturally he had strong motivations for serving.

It was now early January 1944 and with one 'special exercise' over Paris to start off their operational experience, the crew left Upper Heyford behind them for good and moved north to RAF Wigsley. Right on the very fringes of Nottinghamshire and Lincolnshire this little-known airfield served as a flying training school for all but two months of the war and as such saw its fair share of accidents. It was also unofficially remembered rather morbidly as the 'cemetery with lights'. Aircraft production at the time turned out enough Lancasters for active squadrons, but there were not enough to fill 'Heavy' training units. So the crew were obliged to take their conversion course on the much maligned Short Stirling bomber, which was now out of main-force bombing operations. The Stirling was a mixed bag of fruit. She was without a doubt a magnificent-looking machine, was incredibly manoeuvrable, and spacious too. But to an untrained pilot she was a difficult beast to handle, particularly on take-offs and landings. Maurice now had a new engineer to assist him in managing the throttle controls, that helped reduce the customary swings to port, and the four massive radial engines. Only twenty years old, Russell Leggitt from Lowestoft was a

Left John Isfan and sister Persida.
Nick Isfan

Right John Isfan and family.
Nick Isfan

delightful and cheerful-looking young man with a flair for artistry. His hands were his gift and he used them well while operating the gigantic Stirling. The crew flew an unusually high number of hours on the type and remained at Wigsley for a period of eleven weeks before they moved with their newly commissioned pilot to No. 5 Lancaster Finishing School at RAF Syerston in Nottinghamshire.

After a sum total of fourteen hours and ten days spent at Syerston, the crew's logbooks were checked and endorsed by both the flight commander and the chief instructor. They were now all considered competent to fly in and operate the Lancaster bomber. The boys were no doubt happy and relieved to know that wherever they went and whatever was expected of them, they would almost certainly be flying the Lanc. After seven months of rigorous training, the crew were now ready to be posted to an operational squadron. On Saturday 22 April they arrived at RAF Bardney just in time to watch their new squadron mount a night raid to Brunswick in Germany. It was a chaotic and frightening introduction to operational life. Sixteen Lancasters were scheduled to become airborne that night but only three managed to get off

the ground before the fourth swung wildly on take-off. The undercarriage gave way and the bomber skidded across the runway before coming to a halt. The crew made a mad scramble for safety before the fully laden bomber blew up with such spectacular results that some of the locals were seen to be scurrying out of their houses with their belongings. The runway was littered with wreckage and the remaining bombers returned to their dispersals. The three already in the air, and perhaps oblivious to the commotion on the ground, continued on to their target but only two of them returned. Two nights later the city of Munich was the object of No. 9 Squadron's attentions. It was considered a success in the squadron records but this was probably of little comfort to the family of Squadron Leader Brian Gilmore, DFC, who rests quietly with his crew in Durnbach cemetery. One wonders what impressions these first few nights at Bardney had on our fledgling crew.

With scarcely four days to settle in, Maurice – or 'Bunny' as he was now affectionately known – was scheduled to fly as a second pilot on a trip to Schweinfurt. Referred to throughout the RAF as 'second dickey' trips, new pilots were given the opportunity to tag along with an experienced crew and witness at first hand the spectacular sights and sounds of an operation without actually having to take any active involvement. In fact the crew were much happier when they didn't. They just sat in the engineer's fold-down seat and watched the operation develop, keeping a sharp lookout. A spare pair of eyes was always handy. The American 8th Air Force had already bombed the ball-bearing factories at Schweinfurt before in daylight and had suffered appalling losses as a result. That night twenty-one bombers and their crews would not return home; nearly 10% of the aircraft dispatched. Bunny was one of the more fortunate, and after a staggering nine and a half hours in the air, the aircraft and crew landed away at another airfield, due a technical problem. Russell, filling in for another engineer, also came back safely, to the great relief of his crew, who no doubt waited up half the night to welcome their mates home again. As experiences go, perhaps one of the more memorable occurred on the last scheduled raid of April when twelve Lancasters from No. 9 attacked a munitions factory to the north-west of Bordeaux in France. The raid had been called off the night before, even though the bombers were already circling their target. This time Maurice, on his last flight as second pilot, watched the target disappear beneath a series of enormous explosions that lit up the night sky for many miles around. Bernie too watched the devastating display from the bubble of his mid-upper turret, the other aircraft clearly silhouetted against the sea of flames below him. What a sight it would have been.

After eight days at Bardney, the crew were no doubt eager to get on ops. Russell and Bernard had already chalked up a trip each on different nights and with different crews. On the very first day of the month, it was John's turn to take up his position as a replacement bomb aimer for another crew. The practice of poaching men from other crews was universally disliked as there was always the likelihood they wouldn't return and this had emotional as well as practical implications for a group of men who had spent nearly every waking hour for the last six months in each other's company. John went to Toulouse in France late at night, bombed an aircraft repair plant from 5,500 feet and came home again. In fact they all did, which was nothing short of a miracle, given the intensity of flak encountered over the target area. If only this was the shape of things to come. Sadly it wasn't. The following night, Wednesday 3 May, Maurice and crew were finally on the squadron battle order and the target was an obscure place in France by the name of Mailly-le-Camp. On paper it looked straightforward enough and many squadron commanders passed the target off as little more than a milk run. As was often the case, though, one simple sequence of events quickly turned what ought to have been an uneventful trip into a disaster of epic proportions. That night there was a three-quarter moon and little or no cloud cover. The bombing run was delayed and instead of clear precise instructions over the radios, the frequency was flooded with the sounds of American jazz music. A bright-yellow marker flare deliberately drew the circling bombers in like moths to a porch light. It also attracted the German night fighters in great numbers, and in a very short space of time the ground around Mailly was littered with the burning wrecks of forty-odd bombers.

While the raid was considered a success, the colossal number of missing aircraft and men marred the final results. As a consequence of the losses the command decided to alter the rather ludicrous policy that one French raid only constituted a third of a conventional one. Presumably one was more likely to die over Germany than anywhere else. Flying Officer James Ineson and four of his crew bucked the statistics and went down to the north-west of the target. There was no time to dwell on the loss of colleagues. In a little under three weeks three crews had gone, but the eternal optimism of youth precluded the average youngster from ever contemplating his own demise. It always happened to someone else. Three days after Mailly, No. 9

Squadron sent twelve more of its Lancasters to destroy an ammunition dump at Sablé-sur-Sarthe. It was a small concentrated raid and quite unlike the earlier massed operations over Germany involving hundreds upon hundreds of bombers. This time only sixty-eight aircraft took part. Maurice was there just before three in the morning and at 7,000 feet John released the bombload of their Lancaster into the inferno below. As they left, the crew witnessed a series of explosions, some so powerful that debris from the site was tossed up as high as 6,000 feet. Maurice, from a family of committed Christians, would have drawn an enormous amount of pride and relief in knowing that the targets he was hitting at that time were of immediate strategic importance to the war effort. There was no psychological agenda here and bombers operated in smaller numbers and at decreased altitudes to improve accuracy and, it was hoped, greatly reduce civilian casualties on the ground. There was a price to pay, though, and since aircrew were operating at relatively low altitudes, the chances of escaping in their aircraft safely were often much diminished as a result.

The last two trips had been hairy, especially Lille the night before. Two groups of ground crew had waited patiently at their dispersals for the arrival of their charges and crews. They would wait in vain. As was often the way in Bomber Command, one crew were just beginning their tour of operations and the others were very nearly finishing theirs. Experience went a long way in improving your chances of survival, but if you didn't have luck you didn't have much hope. This time, every available Lancaster at Bardney would be bombed up ready to attack a military camp in Belgium. Even though it was late at night, the usual group of well-wishers had assembled at the threshold of the runway and waved each aircraft off. Within about twenty minutes the last of the bombers had disappeared into the dark sky and the deafening sounds of 76 Merlin engines were soon reduced to silence. Just before midnight the leading elements of the 450 bombers committed had reached the Dutch coastline. There were three targets that night and the bombers would split into their respective streams and head south. No. 9 had been designated to fly to Bourg-Leopold. The other targets were the railyards at Leuven and Hasselt. It was becoming increasingly hazy over the target area and although half the

aircraft were capable of dropping their bombs, the remaining eight were told to call off the attack amid fears of civilian casualties. Strangely, Maurice wasn't one of them, nor was he even over the target area when the order to cease bombing came through. In fact, he was thirty-odd miles away to the south-west, and was circling over Leuven when his luck finally ran out at twenty-seven minutes past midnight.

Maurice's parents didn't have long to wait before word reached them. By lunchtime the following day, Fred and Joy had already received the dreaded telegram. To some extent at least, Joy's experiences the night before had prepared them both for the agony of the next few days. The initial shock didn't last long. The uncertainty was far worse. Ron Watson's youngest sister Jean could well remember how utterly devastated her mother was, not just with the early information itself, but also with the prospect of waiting for many weeks and months without definitive news. You didn't dare hope, as that tempted fate, but you couldn't properly grieve either. Though only a boy at the time, Nick Isfan can still see his parents sitting by their wireless, anxious for some news of their son. It did come eventually and in the most unorthodox way. Four months after the boys had been lost, each family received a handwritten letter from a Reverend Henry Willemot of Leuven. A Roman Catholic priest in training and a native of Belgium, Henry had not only heard the final moments of the Lancaster, he had also – at great personal risk – retrieved each body and in turn buried them all within the walls of the monastery close by. The actions of Henry and his colleagues sent the German authorities into a blind rage, as it was expressly forbidden for any civilians to tamper with crash sites. On this occasion at least, common sense and humility prevailed and no further action was taken. Henry's selflessness and sense of duty did not end there. He hoped that by writing to each family individually he could in some small measure bring them comfort. Knowing that he had buried them with the care and attention they so rightly deserved also helped numb the pain. It would not have been an easy task and no doubt the priest concealed the true horrors of the sights he witnessed that night.

Henry closed his letter with the most touching passage: 'I am very happy, dear madam, dear sir, to have been able to render you and him this service. I assure you also that I prayed to the Lord to grant him eternal rest and to give you the courage to bear Christianly this cruel loss, with the hope of seeing your relative again in heaven for ever. Yours sincerely, H. Willemot S.I.'

The deaths of these young men were keenly felt for a very long time. Even now, after so many years, that sense of loss endures. John Leggitt was only twelve when his brother failed to return, but the loss was such that he later travelled to Belgium with his fam-

against the marriage. They were much too young in the first place and, besides, there was a war on. She would eventually make a new life for herself in America, but she kept in touch with Bernie's parents until they passed away. For the remainder of her life a portrait of her first love was never far from her; she would never forget him. Joy Bunnagar could not bring herself to see her son's grave. She wanted to remember him as he was. Fred went in her place and paid his respects to his brave young son. Brother Alan would always remember the last time he saw his

**Left
John Chambers, unknown, Maurice Bunnagar, Ron Watson and Russell Leggitt.**
John Leggitt

ily to sit with Russell a while and thank him for his courage. He has since walked along the crumbling runways of Bardney and perhaps felt his brother's presence. But only he knows that. Nick Isfan was not yet seven when his eldest brother died, so there is little personal heartache. There is, however, a deep sense of pride and admiration for his brother that remains un-dimmed after nearly seventy years. Cynthia Easterlow became a widow at nineteen, but Bernie's parents took her in and loved her as their own, in spite of the fact that they were strongly

brother. As the train pulled away from Lime Street Station in Liverpool, Maurice opened up one of the carriage windows and waved a white handkerchief. Alan laughed; it was so typical of his brother. In time, youngest sibling Ralph would also travel to Belgium with his son, who also carries his uncle's name. Ralph remains philosophical about his brother's death and perhaps by his own admission is a little hardened to it as well. At any rate, he doesn't feel so badly about it now. For he knows he will see him again when the time is right. ●

CHAPTER THREE

UNBEKANNT FLIEGER

BY MARC HALL

THE CANADIAN-BUILT LANCASTER KB713 OF NO. 419 SQUADRON FAILED TO RETURN TO RAF MIDDLETON SAINT GEORGE ON THE NIGHT OF 12/13 MAY 1944, FOLLOWING A RAID TO THE RAIL YARDS AND JUNCTIONS AT LOUVEN (LOUVAIN), A SMALL TOWN IN BELGIUM. A PREVIOUS STRIKE ON THE EVENING OF 11 MAY HAD PRODUCED DISAPPOINTING RESULTS, SO A LARGE FORCE OF RAF HEAVY BOMBERS WAS SENT TWO NIGHTS LATER TO SMASH A TARGET, DEEMED ESSENTIAL IN THE RUN-UP TO THE FORTHCOMING INVASION. THE ENTIRE SEVEN-MAN CREW OF PILOT OFFICER BURDEL EDWARDS'S LANCASTER WOULD PERISH THAT NIGHT. EACH NOW RESTS IN A BELGIAN CEMETERY – THEIR INDIVIDUAL LIVES AND STORIES PREMATURELY ENDED.

PATHFINDERS ILLUMINATED the target at Louvain at approximately 0026 hours. The main force arrived a few minutes later. The full attack opened at 0030, and was over fifteen minutes later, and this time the results appeared to be considerably better, with plenty of damage to the rail network and sheds. But there had been losses. A total of five heavy bombers failed to return, with many lives on the ground sacrificed. Lancaster KB713 did not make it to the target, shot down not far from the French coast with the loss of all its crew.

Sometime before 2200 hours the seven airmen had boarded the aircraft, settling into their positions, with the pilot and flight engineer carrying out their pre-start-up checks under the dim lights in the cockpit. The first of the four Rolls-Royce engines turned over, then slowly popped and spluttered into life, the three other motors following until all were smoothly running in rhythm. Permission was given to taxi to the runway and join the queue of waiting aircraft.

A quick flash of a green Aldis lamp gave the all clear and KB713 lined up on the runway for the last time. Flying Officer Edwards pushed the throttles forward, countered the swing and the Lancaster left the ground, climbing into the dark night sky and gradually gaining altitude. Flight time was estimated at 4 hours 40 minutes with the crew due back at 0240 hours the following morning.

As they crossed the French coast the crew ran into trouble, receiving the attention of a prowling twin-engined Ju88 night fighter, which opened fire on the lumbering bomber, still heavily laden with fuel and bombs. KB713, almost certainly set ablaze, reddening the night sky, was believed to have fallen to the guns of Unteroffizier Martin Siegel from 11/NJG2, between 0045 and 0100 hours near Dunkirk at a height of 2,400 metres. The burning Lancaster slammed into the soft ground of a farmer's field close to the Yser canal, exploding in a large fireball with substantial parts of the aircraft burying themselves deep into the ground. The result was a sizeable crater 12 metres deep. The entire crew were killed, it appears unable to escape the falling aircraft.

Following the end of the Second World War the loss of these men was investigated by sections of the Missing Research and Enquiry Service, led by Squadron Leader P. E. Laughton-Bramley. The crash site was located at Reninge, Belgium, and it was established from the eyewitnesses and local villagers that the aircraft had its bombload on board when it hit the ground, causing an almighty explosion. When the investigating officer visited the town on 28 February 1946, four eyewitnesses were interrogated, including the former pro-German Burgomaster, the former pro-German secretary of the town hall, and cemetery wardens. All declared that on the night in question a four-engined bomber had impacted at Hameau de Knokke, Reninge, from the direction of

Opposite
Original grave marker in Reninge.
Frank Raeman, Belgium

Left
Harold Engman Oddan.
Canadian National Archives

the coast. The witnesses thought that an anti-aircraft battery had shot the aircraft down; however, captured German documents showed the aircraft had been claimed by a night fighter at 0100 hours. An extract from the German records stated the following: 'Lancaster shot down by a night fighter on 13-05-44 at 0100 hours at Reninge, 10 Km South West of Dixmuden. The aircraft crashed and exploded with the bombload, 100% destroyed. Only parts of bodies were found, all crew probably dead.'

What remained of the crew had been collected by the villagers, the same day as the crash, and buried in three small wooden coffins in grave No. 16 in the British plot at Reninge Military Cemetery. Two days later the upper body of a deceased airman was found, the identification disc showing 'R.118580 SMITH,

R.S. RCAF'. The body was taken by the Germans and buried on 16 May in the Military Cemetery at Coxyde, located in West-Vlaanderen, and placed in a single grave at the end of a row of British soldiers killed in 1940. An exhumation at this cemetery confirmed that the remains were those of Flight Sergeant Smith. The aircrew buried at Reninge in the three coffins were located in the corner of the cemetery, a small gap being cut from the boundary hedge to make room for the grave. A small wooden cross with a Union Jack painted on it read 'unbekannt fliegers 13 mai 1944'. A number of items were recovered including parts of the navigator's bag, engine number plates and clothing.

locals in the Reninge area were caring for the grave; it was placed out of the way up against a tool shed. The request for the grave to be moved was turned down, the War Graves Commission responding: 'Where so many relatives are concerned, there is bound to be some difference in the wishes expressed. Many applications for removal have been made, and had to be refused for it is necessary, even if sometimes difficult, for the Commission to follow a consistent line of equality to all. It is not a question of trouble or expense but simply adherence to a rule of action which is generally accepted, and the dissatisfaction which would result if different decisions were made in different cases can be readily visualised.' However,

In July 1947, Reverend Harvey Campbell and his wife Grace Campbell (the famous novelist), the parents of twins Robert and Alexander, travelled from Canada to the continent via London to visit the graves of both of their sons – Flying Officer Robert Roy Campbell and Pilot Officer Alexander Campbell were both killed in action within five weeks of each other. They visited Reninge and found the collective grave containing the mixed remains of six airmen. At the time the grave was being cared for by a resident of Brugge (twenty miles away) named Yvonne Hermans who attended on a regular basis to lay flowers. Reverend Campbell asked that the remains be moved to Adegem as the men buried there were Canadians and continued care would be simpler. It appeared no

the Commission's reply also stated that an inquiry would be launched into the concern and that the grave would not be left in its present location if it was not possible to ensure a high standard of maintenance. Clearly further action was taken as the remains of the six crew who were buried in Reninge Military Cemetery do now rest in a collective grave in Adegem Canadian War Cemetery, the exhumation and relocation taking place in 1968.

The aircraft's navigator was Flying Officer Robert Roy Campbell, one of three sons to Reverend Harvey and Grace Campbell. Robert was born on 7 October 1922 in Glengarry, Ontario, and left full-time education at Regina College to join the RCAF on 13 December 1941, requesting flying duties, preferably as a pilot but willing to fill other aircrew positions. At No. 2 Initial Training School he scored extremely well in all subjects, with a total of 91.4%, and he was highly recommended as having the ability and temperament to be a navigator, noted as a 'leading student in his flight'. Later, in July 1942, he began an air navigators' course at the No. 3 Air Observers School in Regina and again scored well in his exams. Robert was described by the chief instructor as having a 'very pleasing personality and he gets along well with his fellows'. Having been awarded his navigator's badge on 23 October 1942 and at the same time promoted to sergeant, Robert left Canada in December

assessed as being potential observer material, with continual refreshment in mathematical subjects, and he should be considered for active duties as aircrew. He succeeded in passing the air bombers' course on 23 May 1943 at the No. 7 Air Observers School, although the chief instructor recorded that he could have applied himself better, was a little lax, and at times lacked self-drive. Arriving in the UK on his birthday in 1943, Peter spent many months advancing his skills before finally being posted for active service on 16 March 1944 just a few months before he was killed. His commission to the rank of pilot officer was received two days prior to his death. He left behind a wife whom he had married in June 1941, Kathleen

Left to Right Joseph Alexander Webber; Roy Stanley Smith; Peter Dewar; Robert Roy Campbell. *Canadian National Archives*

1942 for the UK and, following further training, and possibly some time instructing, he was posted to No. 419 Squadron on 16 March 1944 to begin operations.

Pilot Officer Peter Dewar was born on 1 July 1914 in Lethbridge, Alberta, one of three siblings to Thomas and Janet Dewar. Peter's parents had both been born, and married, in Stirling, Scotland. Prior to enlisting in July 1942 he had spent time in various occupations, including that of stenographer, clerk, ore sorter and a carpenter's assistant. Recorded as very quiet, with a sincere manner, Peter had been an athletic type, playing hockey, baseball and rugby extensively. The general medical board was of the opinion that he would have trouble with the studying as it was eight years since he had left school. Peter, however, was

Mary, and two young sons, Thomas and Donald.

The airman manning the Lancaster's wireless set was Pilot Officer Roy Stanley Smith of Ontario, Canada. Born on 11 October 1922 to Violet and Blake Smith, Roy was one of three siblings, having two brothers and a sister. Following his early school years, Roy attended Hamilton Technical School studying industrial electrics, while holding down a job as a delivery boy with Dominion Stores Ltd. Following three years as a packer with Balfours Ltd, Roy became a machine operator with the Boston Insulated Wire and Cable Company, and studied at a machine-shop course at Westdale Technical night school in his spare time. In March 1941 Roy offered his services to the RCAF. Clearly having an interest and background in technical matters and machines, Roy enlisted as an airframe mechanic, subsequently volunteering for flying duties towards the end of 1942. One of his three references, while working as a mechanic, stated: 'I have known Roy Stanley Smith and his family for many years. His father was decorated for bravery in the last war and this young man has the same brave spirit of his sire. I can vouch for his honesty, trustworthiness and cheerful disposition. He is a bright and intelligent man, keen on mechanics and undoubtedly would be a great asset in any branch of the Royal Canadian Air Force.' Roy made it clear that he had an interest in radio and had carried out minor repairs. He was intent on an aircrew position

Right
Burdel Frank
Edwards.
Canadian National Archives

and so 'wireless operator' was the perfect trade. Roy was remustered as aircrew and undertook a course at the No. 4 Wireless School, his examiners marking him as 'above average'. It was from here that he went on to No. 2 Gunnery School, gaining comments such as 'academically above average'. It was also noted that Roy was 'quite aggressive' in his approach and that he was a 'hard worker'. After finishing his training in Canada, Roy was posted overseas and left Halifax, Nova Scotia, on 16 July 1943, arriving at Greenock in Scotland on 22 July 1943. More time was spent honing his skills at No. 11 Radio School and he finally joined No. 419 Squadron on 16 March 1944, having completed a heavy bomber conversion course and training sorties with No. 22 Operational Training

Unit. Only two days before he was killed a promotion was issued to the rank of pilot officer. Roy never married but did leave behind an English girlfriend.

Flying Officer Joseph Alexander Webber was one of the Lancaster's air gunners, manning the small cramped turret defending the aircraft from attack. He was born on 27 March 1913 in Manitoba and was one of the older members of the crew. Coming from a large family, residing in Calgary, Joseph was one of seven children to Joseph and Sarah Webber. Joseph junior had undertaken an apprenticeship, following in the footsteps of his father, as a paperhanger and painter. He was initially employed and taught by his father, spending six years with him up until 1935. He then went to work at Crossland and Beale, a painting contractor business, until 1941. A family man, Joseph had three young sons and a wife, Lillian, whom he married on 13 March 1937 in Sarcee, Alberta.

Joseph joined the RCAF in June 1941 as a security guard and was posted to Penhold Alberta Manning Depot carrying out general security tasks. The following year he sought air gunner duties and he impressed his interview board, his report mentioning that he was 'anxious to get in aircrew and should make a good air gunner'. His personnel officer stated: 'Education suitable, class score very good. This airman might make observer or pilot with a short education course.' Having made it through the selection board, Joseph enrolled on a gunnery course with the No. 8 Gunnery School in Lethbridge on 5 July 1942 and was awarded the air gunner's badge on 25 September 1942 before going on to an instructing school. He was assessed as being competent as a gunnery instructor and spent time teaching at Macdonald. It was not until December 1943 that he was finally posted overseas.

Following the heavy conversion course, Joseph was sent with his crew to No. 419 Squadron for operational duty. Less than eight weeks later he was missing. His wife, Lillian, remained optimistic. In a letter to an RCAF casualty officer, dated 10 March 1945, she wrote: 'Dear Sirs, In answer to your letter for information concerning my husband, Flying Officer Joseph Alexander Webber, I have had no news concerning him and I wish to thank you for your kind sympathy in the past and now. I will not let my hopes down for his safe return until this fight is over. I am yours sincerely, Mrs Lillian Webber.'

Flying Officer Harold Engman Oddan, the other air gunner on board KB713, was born in Manitoba on 12 March 1911, one of three sons to Ole and Mary Oddan. They also had six daughters. Harold's was a farming background, like many of the young men who enlisted from the prairie regions. His father owned and ran a farm on which Harold worked from 1928 to 1935, then departing to run his own farm, which he would leave behind when he enlisted in the RCAF in 1941. Harold was keen on flying duties, as either a wireless operator or air gunner. The selection board found him suitable for both trades, commenting: 'Physical efficiency tests – fit. A quick acting and attentive chap. … Sound rural type, keen intelligence, alert and mature.' Harold, however, struggled on the wireless operators' course in Calgary, which he had started in March 1942. It appeared he could not cope with Morse code. He was soon transferred to air gunner training and was awarded the air gunner's badge on 20 November 1942. It was a year before he was posted overseas, having spent time instructing, the commanding officer at one course stating: 'He has completed the No. 9 Gunnery Instructors (Aircrew) Course finishing 4th in a class of 12. A keen hard working pupil showing interest throughout the course. His armament knowledge is good and with further experience he will develop a good lecturing ability. He will make a good assistant instructor.' Harold was married to Adrianna on 18 April 1942 while in service, and it was not long before she fell pregnant with their first and only child. Sharon was born on 7 September 1943 only eight months before Harold was killed.

Unfortunately little is known about the crew's flight engineer, Sergeant John Robert Carruthers of the Royal Air Force Volunteer Reserve.

The skipper of the crew, believed to have been a skilled and capable pilot, was Flying Officer Burdel Frank Edwards. Born on 12 December 1919 in Bloomington, a small village in Grant County, Wisconsin, USA, Burdel's parents divorced when he was a young boy and he was cared for by his maternal grandparents. When he was six his mother remarried and he moved in with her and his stepfather. Burdel was schooled locally at the Bloomington public school from 1925 before moving on to the high school and leaving the twelfth grade in 1937. It was in the same year that he undertook a commercial

pilots' course. On completion of the course he became a flight instructor for the next two years and in 1940 settled down as a crop-dusting pilot in Texas, with plenty of low-level single-engined flying. When he applied for the RCAF he already had 700 hours of flying experience and was an accomplished pilot.

Burdel impressed the interview board, a note stating that with guidance he would make 'a bloody good pilot'. It seemed, however, that he had difficulty with authority and he mentioned to the interviewing officer that he was washed out of the US Air Corps due to disciplinary reasons. The interviewing officer commented that Burdel appeared to have a lack of self-control, a fast temper and was hard to manage. Indeed, discipline issues would arise. Throughout October 1943 to January 1944, while stationed with No. 24 Operational Training Unit, charges were made relating to the paying of mess bills and loans to airmen with cheques that were later dishonoured when trying to cash them. The total value was approximately £60. Burdel suffered a severe reprimand and forfeiture of seniority.

Burdel carried out his service elementary flight training in Oshawa, Ontario, and from there went to service flight training in Hagersville, Ontario, finally being awarded his wings on 5 March 1943. His flight training had been interrupted and took longer than normal owing to hospitalisation, and he had been put back a course. After being posted abroad he was sent to an Advanced Flying Unit and Operational Training Unit where he crewed up and completed further training, such as fighter affiliation and cross-countries, and then conversion to the four-engined Avro Lancaster. In Burdel's record the following has been noted upon completion of the AFU training: 'Average in his flying and preflight work. Rather slow starting the course but has improved a great deal. Good average Captain. He has carried out four day cross countries and six night cross countries at an average height of 14,000 including one Bull's-eye and one Pickle. Four details of fighter affiliation with Tomahawks and decompression chamber exercises. He will have no difficulty in converting to the four engined aircraft but may require a little more dual than average. A good pilot who at times appears to be overconfident.' When Burdel lost his life on the operation to Louvain, he left behind a wife, Francis May, whom he had married on 22 November 1942.●

CHAPTER FOUR

SAINT TROND – A CHANCE MEETING

BY MARC HALL

IN THE EARLY HOURS OF FRIDAY 28 APRIL 1944 THE FAMILIAR DRONING SOUND OF HEAVY BOMBERS COULD BE HEARD BY THOSE FAR BELOW. RAF BOMBER COMMAND WAS SENDING HUNDREDS OF LANCASTERS AND HALIFAXES, LADEN WITH THOUSANDS OF GALLONS OF FUEL AND THOUSANDS OF POUNDS OF BOMBS, INTO THE DARK SKY, HEADING EAST. NUMEROUS TARGETS HAD BEEN DESIGNATED, INCLUDING THE RAIL YARDS AT MONTZEN, DETAILED AS PART OF THE AIR PLAN TO SUPPORT THE FORTH-COMING D-DAY LANDINGS. FOR ONE OF THE CREWS CHOSEN TO ATTACK THE TARGET THAT NIGHT, MADE UP OF SEVEN CANADIANS AND ONE BRITON, IT WAS TO BE THEIR FINAL FLIGHT. THEY WOULD NOT BE RETURNING HOME.

THE MAIN TARGET for the night of 27/28 April 1944 was the military factories at Friedrichshafen, but other raids were detailed in an attempt to keep the night fighters from the main bombing force. These smaller attacks included targets at Montzen in Belgium and Aulnoye in France, together with another diversionary raid by Operational Training Unit aircraft over the North Sea towards Jutland.

At 2323 hours on 27 April Canadian Bomber Command pilot John Gilson pushed the throttles fully forward and the four Hercules motors roared under the strain. Slowly the heavily laden bomber lumbered down the runway, gathering speed, leaving British soil for the last time. With a belly full of high explosives and fuel, MZ536 slowly gained height. On board, the vibrations from the four power plants ran through the fuselage as the motors steadied into a constant drone and the crew settled to their tasks. The target for this particular crew was the busy marshalling and railway yards at Montzen, located in eastern Belgium and a short distance from the German border.

H-hour was planned for 0130, the raid consisting of three separate waves of aircraft, the second and third of which were to suffer the heaviest losses. It appears that there were delays with the assembling of the enemy night fighters and most of the first wave managed to evade their attention. The night-fighter controllers were confronted with four separate bomber streams, and it took some time before they could coordinate an adequate response against the intruders. Once the possible route of the bombers was established, a number of night fighters were sent at speed towards Aachen, to the north-east of the marshalling yards. But most arrived too late and by 0144 hours the raid was over, with the stream already heading for home and the target in flames. However, as the main bomber force withdrew, the German night fighters began to mount a ferocious and effective response against the bomber stream. A number of the interceptors were being flown by Nachtjagdgeschwader 1 aces who had taken off as the raiders flew past Saint Trond. A meeting was being held nearby in which a number of high-ranking night-fighter aces and commanders were attending, and when the alarm was sounded they responded.

Many Bomber Command airmen were to lose their lives at the hands of these experienced pilots, some of whom pursued their foe out across the North Sea. The night fighters managed to shoot down fifteen of the heavy bombers: fourteen Halifaxes and one Lancaster failed to return that night. One of these was Halifax MZ536, with the loss of all of the crew. As the four-engined Halifax neared the target, Dale Loewen, bomb aimer on MZ536, had issued directions to the pilot, with the bomb doors open. With bombs released, target photograph taken and bomb doors closed, the crew now had one objective: set course for home and get there as quickly and safely as possible. Approximately forty minutes after H-hour, however, the bomber came within the sights of a stalking Messerschmitt Bf110 G4 interceptor, captained by Oberleutnant Georg-Hermann Greiner, of II/NGJ1. From below and behind, most likely unseen under the cover of darkness, the Bf110's guns opened up and riddled the aircraft. The fate of the bomber and its crew was sealed. It was the second victory of the night for the night-fighter ace Greiner – his twenty-third claim.

It is likely that the unsuspecting crew never knew what hit them. There was an instant fire in one of the wings, the fuel was ablaze, the surrounding night sky

Left John Gilson
Courtesy of Russ and Fred Buglas

illuminated. Even if the night fighter had been seen, it appears it had been too late for anything to be done about it. With the Halifax – then at approximately 4,200 metres – engulfed in flames, the aircraft immediately began falling. One can only surmise that those inside stood little prospect of escape. The aircraft was witnessed plummeting from the sky at 0212 hours – a large red fireball plunging earthwards, hitting the ground and exploding with great force, completely destroying it, and scattering wreckage. The place of the crash was 1km to the north-west of a small village named Trognée in Belgium. Sometime afterwards the

130; Airman 'Vorsith' (also shown as 'Forsith'), grave 131; Airman Holloway, grave 132; Flying Officer Loewen, grave 133; Sergeant Hanson, grave 134; two unknown airmen, graves 135 and 136.

The information was relayed back to the Air Ministry via an International Red Cross telegram quoting German information. As there was no 'Airman Holloway' in this crew, and this name was not identified as a casualty anywhere within the Air Ministry's files, he was assumed to be another 'unknown' until he could be identified and the case of the missing crew could

Right The seven-man Halifax crew. Unfortunately the picture was never annotated, but Dale Loewen is confirmed as back row far right and John Gilson as back row second from the right.
Courtesy of Russ and Fred Buglas

remains of the crew and wreckage were cleared from the site and the airmen were buried two days later on 30 April 1944 in the Fort Borsbeek Antwerpen-Deurne cemetery. (There was another cemetery at Saint Trond, near Trognée, but the salvage team came from another base in Belgium. This may explain the distance between the crash site and the burial location.) The Germans were unable to correctly identify all of the crew and the 'Totenlist' or death list number 219 recorded: Sergeant Greig (also shown as 'Grnid'), grave 129; Sergeant Wilson, grave

be cleared up by the Missing Research and Enquiry Service. When the investigation was carried out – taking into account that five airmen were identified and that the Halifax had a crew of eight – these three unknown men were assumed to be part of that crew. The bodies were eventually exhumed from their original graves and reburied in December 1945 in the Antwerp Schoonselhof Cemetery, Wilrijk, a suburb of Antwerp, Belgium.

The raid proved to be only partially successful. Just

the eastern parts of the railway yards were hit, with destruction and damage to railway tracks, sheds, storage depots and a good number of locomotives and wagons. Even so, the rail yards were up and running again on 10 May.

The eight-man crew of MZ536 had been with No. 431 Squadron since 13 March 1944. The bomb aimer was Flying Officer Dale Howard Loewen, born on 30 October 1920 in the small town of Scott, Saskatoon, to John and Catherine Loewen – one of six siblings, Dale was the youngest son. Coming from a horticultural background, Dale continued working as a labourer after leaving school in 1937 but he had his sights set on aviation and secured an opportunity to study aeronautics at a technical school in Saskatoon with the Royal Canadian Air Force. He enlisted as ground crew and qualified as an air-frame mechanic, a profession he continued with until late 1942 when he volunteered for aircrew. Attending his assessments in June 1942 he was said to be 'alert', and of 'good material' and so started training with No. 7 Air Observer School in Portage-la-Prairie, Manitoba, receiving his commission on 25 June 1943. He scored well in the exams but was found unsuitable for the role of navigator and so transferred to the bomb-aimers'

course, his assessors recording, 'Good type lad. Above average intelligence. A bit torn down after flunking out at the Air Observers School but should equal to the task of air bomber if he gets down to work.' He was subsequently found to be above average, and at the end of July 1943 he embarked aboard a ship in Halifax, bound for the UK, arriving at the beginning of August. Following further training he was sent to No. 82 Operational Training Unit, prior to a transfer to No. 431 Squadron.

Pilot Officer Richard William Pratt was the aircraft's wireless operator. Born on 1 June 1911 in Quebec, Richard was one of the older members of the crew. He had four sisters and two brothers. His younger brother died in 1924, and his father passed away in 1935. Following school Richard worked with the International Paper and Pulp Company as a logger. In his spare time he played softball, baseball and hockey, and seemed to enjoy the outdoor life. He had applied to the RCAF on 5 December 1939 and was told to wait, but he reapplied and was enlisted on 11 June 1940 for ground duties as an equipment assistant. Not content Richard requested to be trained for aircrew, as a gunner, stating he was not accustomed to working indoors. Following several failed applications

Left Dale Loewen.
Courtesy of Russ and Fred Buglas

Left Dale Loewen and John Gilson.
Courtesy of Russ and Fred Buglas

he was finally successful.

Richard trained at No. 2 Wireless School from 8 December 1941 through to 22 June 1942 and came forty-second out of seventy-three in the class with a score of 74.3% – 'average ability'. He was sent on a gunnery course in July 1942, coming fourth in the class and earning comments from his instructors including 'dependable' and 'ground training very satisfactory'. Leaving Canada for the United Kingdom in January 1943 he finally arrived at No. 103 Squadron, but eleven days later was sent to No. 487 Squadron where he remained until October 1943. His next posting was to No. 82 Operational Training Unit prior to arrival at No. 431 Squadron.

The rear gunner – one of the loneliest jobs in the crew – was Pilot Officer John Wilson, a Scottish national born on 19 July 1923 in Possilpark, Glasgow. He was one of four children to John and Margaret Wilson. Six years after his birth the family emigrated to Canada and settled in Toronto. Following schooling John took a job as a bus boy at the Royal York Hotel, where he stayed until April 1941, leaving to work for

the Dunlop Rubber Company. A short time later, in May 1941, he volunteered for the RCAF as an air gunner. Following training, in which he scored 74% on his final exam, he left Canada and arrived in the UK on 19 September 1943 to undertake further instruction with No. 82 Operational Training Unit. Flying mainly on Wellingtons, and building up a total of 82.25 flying hours, John impressed his instructors, his senior armament officer remarking: 'Quite good results. Willing to work hard, a very good type.' Prior to his death John had only taken part in six operations with the squadron, including the raid to Montzen. His mother appeared to be unaware that her son was actively flying on operations. Perhaps John had not wished to burden her with the reality of war. A handwritten letter from John's mother to the RCAF, dated 25 May 1944, stated: 'Dear Sirs, In reference to file number 198432b (No. 4) will you please give me a little further information regarding my son who is missing after air operations overseas. I did not know that he was flying, he held it back from me to keep me from worrying. Could you please let me know how many operations he had taken part in.'

Right John Gilson, far left, and his Halifax crew.
Courtesy of Russ and Fred Buglas

Pilot Officer Gordon Templeton Greig was another of the air gunners aboard the Halifax, occupying the mid-upper turret. Born in Saskatoon on 3 June 1922 to James and Jessie Greig, Gordon was one of six children, having two brothers and three sisters. Gordon left Fort Frances High School in 1940 to study business at the Brantford Business College in Ontario, following which he started work with the Slingsby Manufacturing Company. Gordon enlisted for flying with the RCAF on 5 November 1942 and it seems he was certainly keen, his interviewing officer commenting: 'Neat, clean cut type, fond of sports, wants aircrew in any capacity.' Having been accepted as an air gunner, Gordon commenced his gunnery course on 12 July 1943, completing it on 20 August. His commanding officer remarked: 'Good student, no difficulty in understanding, but routine worker, not much initiative. Dependable, takes the lead occasionally.' Shortly after, he was posted overseas to the UK, leaving on 13 September 1943. Arriving at No. 82 Operational Training Unit he completed further training on the Wellington, obtaining observations such as 'good crew member, good gunner' from his seniors.

Another of the aircraft's air gunners, the mid-under gunner, was Flight Sergeant George Quist Hansen of Standard, a remote village surrounded by miles of open farmland in Alberta. Born on 6 April 1919 George was the son of Hilda and James Hansen, both Canadian citizens but originally from Sweden and Denmark respectively. George was one of six children, three of his brothers also serving in the armed forces. He completed his education locally and left school in 1933 at the age of fourteen. He helped his father in their family store until 1938 before becoming a miner. He left in 1939 to take up driving positions with two different companies until 1940, finishing as a clerk with a grocery business in 1942. Having enlisted for the RCAF the medical officer's report mentioned 'considerable flying experience as pilot'. George expressed an interest to serve as a pilot or air gunner; however, he was assessed as medically unfit for the role of pilot owing to poor eye muscles. He was sent on a wireless operator's course but it seems he struggled, finding Morse code difficult to grasp, and he missed part of the course when briefly hospitalised. Brought back for reselection in January 1943

Left Richard William Pratt and John Wilson.
Canadian National Archives

Left to right
Gordon Templeton
Greig; George
Quist Hansen;
Thomas Rex
Forsyth. *Canadian*
National Archives

George expressed a desire to be an air gunner, and eventually undertook a gunnery course, faring much better. He qualified on 23 June 1943, his instructor remarking: 'Displays good gunnery sense in the air, obliging, co-operative and should make a capable Air Gunner.' George was posted overseas in July 1943. He left behind a wife, whom he had married on 27 August 1942, and a one-year-old son.

Flying Officer Thomas Rex Forsyth, the aircraft's navigator, was born on 22 October 1912 in Magrath, Alberta, and was one of the older members of the crew. Following his basic education, and work on a farm carrying out general duties, Thomas went on to study philosophy and English at university prior to enlisting with the RCAF on 8 April 1942 in Calgary, Alberta. Thomas's hobbies encompassed skating, swimming and softball, and particularly photograraphy as an amateur and a professional developer. His interviewing officers rated him highly and he scored very well on his assessments, recording, 'His life on the farm has trained him to be constantly on the alert and he can be depended on for clear thinking and prompt decisive action in the event of serious emer-

gencies.' Other comments from his interviewing officer included 'resolute, straight forward and above average air crew'.

Thomas had enlisted with the RCAF because he saw it as an alternative to the Army draft and he preferred the Air Force owing to the better learning opportunities. He held a long-standing interest in flying, although he did mention to his assessors that he felt insecure in the air, but could get used to it. He wanted to be an observer, considering that he was not particularly well equipped to be a pilot. Thomas soon began navigator training and he seemed at home with the theory and practical work. Having qualified as a navigator on 19 March 1943, rated as 'above average', he was commissioned as a pilot officer and posted overseas in April 1943. A further promotion to flying officer was gained on 19 September 1943, and training continued at No. 6 Advanced Flying Unit and No. 82 Operational Training Unit before being taken on strength with No. 431 Squadron on 13 March 1944. Thomas's wife became a widow a few weeks later.

Sergeant Robert Wallace of the Royal Air Force Volunteer Reserve was the flight engineer on the crew.

**Left John Gilson
and his mother
Elizabeth.** *Courtesy of
Russ and Fred Buglas*

Unfortunately nothing more is known regarding this particular airman.

The crew's pilot, Pilot Officer John Gilson, also known as Jack, was born on 20 June 1921 in Traynor, Saskatchewan, the son of Thomas and Elizabeth Gilson. John appears to have been their only son, although he did have two sisters. Recreationally he enjoyed playing hockey and softball. Having worked on a farm he enlisted with the RCAF on 29 October 1940, for ground duties, including truck driving. In early 1941, however, he made an application to remuster for aircrew, and so began the path to become a pilot, starting out on the De Havilland Tiger Moth and progressing to more advanced flying on the Avro Anson. During his elementary flying training, which he finished in April 1942, John was deemed 'average ability', showing a weakness for aerobatics, although it was mentioned that he should do well if he was pushed. John qualified as a pilot, receiving his flying badge on 28 August 1942, and was posted overseas to the UK.

Intensive instruction followed at No. 6 Advanced Flying Unit, from 17 November 1942 until 6 February 1943, on night flying, instrument flying and general-purpose flying. His commanding officer reported him as 'A tough but dependable type who has coped well with the course on the whole, should make a good operational pilot.' John quickly progressed, with two further promotions. He was to receive his commission on 26 April 1944, just two days before he was killed. In 1942 when he was transferred overseas to the UK John had made contact with some of his relatives. During a break in training in 1944 they had all met up at his Aunt Nell's home in Staffordshire for some 'home cooking'. As John was leaving his aunt asked him to 'come back soon'. John had turned to her and said, 'Somehow I don't think I will be.' ◉

**Left John Gilson,
Aunt Nell and
cousins Walter and
Jim Garrett.** *Courtesy
of Russ and Fred Buglas*

CHAPTER FIVE

A WILL AND A WAY

NO TARGET WAS EVER WITHOUT ITS RISKS. GENERALLY, THOUGH, ATTACKING TRANS-PORTATION LINKS SUPPORTING THE INVASION AND FLYING BOMB SITES IN NORTHERN FRANCE WERE CONSIDERED LESS HAZARDOUS THAN A LONG HAUL TO BERLIN, OR THE INTENSE FLAK OF THE 'HAPPY VALLEY'. BUT DANGER STALKED THE MEN OF BOMBER COMMAND WHEREVER THEY FLEW, AND EVEN THE MORE EXPERIENCED MEN TOWARDS THE END OF THEIR FIRST TOUR, AND COMPARATIVE SAFETY, COULD TAKE NOTHING FOR GRANTED.

SHORTLY BEFORE midnight on 6 June 1944, the Kommandeur of II/NJG4, Hauptmann Paul-Hubert Rauh, raced across the tarmac at Châteaudun airfield to his ageing Messerschmitt Bf110 night fighter. There had been high hopes for Willie Messerschmitt's twin-engined 'Zerstorer' ('Destroyer') before the war, but as a day fighter in the Battle of Britain its flaws had been badly exposed. Relegated to a night-time interception role, however, it had excelled. Although better aircraft had superseded its design, and huge antenna and extra equipment had impacted its performance, in the right hands it could be deadly. And with Rauh at the controls it was especially lethal.

His orders were clear: the British were playing havoc with the ground radio control frequencies – the vital link between aircraft and controller – and so he was to fly a 'freelance' sortie in the area of St Lô. And he was in luck. Heading towards him was a large formation of more than 100 Lancasters on its bombing run to destroy road and rail links at Vire and prevent German reinforcements and armour from reaching the beachhead.

Carefully selecting his first target, Rauh eased his fighter into the enemy's blind spot and opened fire, his cannon shells tearing into the moving shadow of a Lancaster in front of him. The heavy bomber almost immediately fell out of the stream and headed crashing to earth. Happily, six out of the seven crew members managed to make it out of the stricken bomber, including its Canadian pilot.

Rauh was pleased with his fifteenth victory, Lancaster ME811 of No. 576 Squadron, but his night's work was not yet done. Minutes later he observed another dark shape in the sky, and identified it immediately as a Lancaster. Sliding once more into position, his thumb hovered over the gun button until his sights rested upon the aircraft's wings and its vulnerable petrol tanks. He opened fire.

Lancaster NE173 of No. 103 Squadron was only moments from destruction; its crew, skippered by another Canadian pilot – Flight Lieutenant Wilfred Way – was on its final sortie.

Wilfred Way, RCAF, always known as 'Bill', had been a bank clerk before the war. Born in Manitoba on 22 October 1920, he had taken naturally to flying and

eased through service training on single and then twin-engined aircraft. Converting to the four-engined Halifax at 1656 Heavy Conversion Unit (HCU) at Lindholme, Bill found himself in charge of a crew that was complete save for a pilot. He could not have hoped for a better group of men.

The navigator was Pilot Officer Derrick Hollingsworth who, like Bill, had been a bank clerk before volunteering for aircrew. Derrick was a Londoner whereas the air bomber, and the third of the three officers in the crew, was a Canadian. Pilot Officer John Gallacher, from Port McNicoll in Ontario, had given up his studies to train for war.

The rest of the crew were non-commissioned men: two Englishmen and one Australian. The two Englishmen were both from Yorkshire: Flight Sergeant Roger Cooper, from Leeds, was the wireless operator; Sergeant John Jennings was the flight engineer. John, from Bradford, was the baby of the group and only nineteen years of age. Conversely, the oldest and final member of their band, the air gunner, was thirty-two. Flight Sergeant Leonard Zingelmann, RAAF, came from Boonah, Queensland, Australia. The bulk of the crew, minus their pilot, had been together since the Operational Training Unit (OTU). The flight engineer had joined at HCU, having been a direct entrant, and completed his training within six months of joining up. He had enlisted on his eighteenth birthday.

In February 1944, with their training over, the crew was posted to No. 103 Squadron at Elsham Wolds, officially arriving on the 9th. Elsham Wolds, in Lincolnshire, had originally been established to help counter the Zeppelin threat in the First World War. By 1944 it was home to two main-force Lancaster squadrons – Nos 103 and 576 – and part of 1 Group under the command of Air Vice-Marshal Edward Rice. By the time the Way crew arrived, the squadron had been stood down for several days as a result of the foul winter weather, much to the annoyance of the pugnacious officer commanding, Wing Commander Eric Nelson. (Nelson, who had boxed for the RAF between 1932 and 1939, later went on to achieve air rank.)

No. 103 had already established a proud tradition of 'pressing on' while others may have faltered, and yet its casualty count was still within the realms of what would have been considered 'acceptable'. Only three crews, for example, had been lost in January,

Right
John Jennings, the
nineteen-year old
flight engineer, had
enlisted on his
eighteenthth
birthday. *Anonymous*

although the weather had mercifully played its part in keeping those losses to a minimum.

As was customary with any new crew, they were not initially let loose on their own, but rather flew as part of a more experienced team to learn their trade. As such, Bill and the two Johns – Gallacher and Jennings – found themselves in the company of Pilot Officer Edgar Jones on the night of 24/25 February for their first taste of true operations, taking part in a thankfully uneventful trip to Schweinfurt. While all of the crews reported the usual flak and searchlights, and at least one had a run-in with an enemy fighter, all of them returned safely. (Jones, who was coming to the end of his operational tour, was awarded the Distinguished Flying Cross at the end of the month.)

The very next night, Jones was reunited with his usual crew and Bill was given the chance to win his spurs, his colleagues being joined by a 'spare bod' in both the rear and the mid-upper turrets (Zingelmann, although on the Battle Order was taken ill). The target was Augsburg, the squadron contributing 9 bombers – a comparatively modest total – to an attacking force of almost 600 on the first major raid to the city.

The raid was a stunning success, but the crew's first operation almost proved to be their last. On two occasions – both on their way in and on their homeward journey – they were attacked by twin-engined night fighters, but both times they were successful in fighting them off. Not so lucky was Flight Lieutenant William Eddy, DSO, who was shot down by flak but managed a forced landing, thus saving himself and all of his crew. Eddy even succeeded in evading capture and making it home. (He later went on to add the DFC to his Distinguished Service Order, flying with No. 139 Squadron Pathfinder Force.)

No doubt buoyed up by their achievement, but similarly disturbed by the attention paid to their aircraft by the German Nachtjäger, the crew (complete with the mid-upper now fully recovered) had to wait another full month before they were again on operations, this time to the 'Big City' – Berlin – on what was to be the last major raid on it of the war. Even to the more experienced crews, the mere mention of this target was enough to have them running to the nearest boys' room. The German capital was understandably heavily defended, and a long way distant, especially from the hinterland of Lincolnshire, often

necessitating an arduous and nerve-wracking homeward leg across the North Sea.

Their payload was substantial, a reflection of their air officer commanding's drive to deliver the heaviest payloads in all of his squadrons' aircraft. The majority carried one 4,000lb 'Cookie' accompanied by six 1,000lb medium-capacity (MC) bombs and the odd 500lb bomb. The remainder conveyed primarily incendiaries, the intention being to blast the roofs from the Germans' buildings and set them ablaze.

Take-off was shortly after 1830 hours, Bill getting away at 1851, one of the last of the squadron's 16 aircraft to leave out of a total attacking force of more than 800. Climbing out, the crew quickly settled into its routine, the bombers assembling over Mablethorpe on the coast to join the stream for the long outward leg. Although the crew did not know it at the time, strong winds were to play havoc on the raid, with almost disastrous consequences. Intense flak over the target and in a belt between Leipzig and Berlin was especially deadly; many aircraft were blown off course and found themselves over the defences of the Ruhr.

John Gallacher, the air bomber, dropped his bombload successfully on the Pathfinder markers at 2251, and with bomb doors closed, the navigator Derrick Hollingsworth gave his skipper the course for home. Almost immediately there was a call from the 'spare bod' rear gunner, Sergeant Jones, to 'corkscrew' – an extreme evasive manoeuvre that put immense pressure on the airframe and crew alike. The gunner had seen what he identified as a Focke Wulf Fw190 while still some 2,000 yards distant, and alerted his pilot shortly before the single-engined fighter opened fire with a long burst. Jones squeezed his guns' triggers, but instead of the comforting sound of his four Browning machine guns and the reassuring smell of cordite, there was nothing; his guns had frozen.

Mid-upper gunner Leonard Zingelmann had better luck, and fired off his own longer burst as the fighter came into his sights at 500 yards. He had the satisfaction of seeing his tracer ammunition find its mark as the Focke Wulf broke away to port. Any euphoria was short-lived, however, for some of the enemy's cannon shells had struck the Lancaster's starboard wing. Fortunately the damage was not serious, although the aeroplane did not make it back to base, the navigator preferring instead to direct his pilot to North Killingholme.

The raid on Berlin had been costly to Bomber Command, seventy-two aircraft being shot down, the majority by flak. One was from No. 103 Squadron, flown by Squadron Leader Kenneth Bickers, DFC. Bickers, a flight commander and only twenty-one years of age, had been awarded the DFC for gallantry for fending off a determined attack by an enemy fighter in April the previous year. But the total loss figure in any raid did not always tell the whole story. Often aircraft would return damaged, with dead or wounded on board. In Flight Sergeant Browning's crew, for example, his rear gunner had been killed in a fighter attack, and the pilot did well to nurse his damaged plane back to crash-land at Dunsfold.

Way and the crew returned to Elsham Wolds in time for the squadron's next operation to Essen in the 'Happy Valley' – as the Ruhr was ironically named – on the night of 26/27 March. It was yet another eventful night for at least three of the crews. The aircraft flown by Flight Sergeant Whitley returned early with engine trouble, and in the resulting crash-landing his aircraft caught fire. Pilot Officer Birchall and Warrant Officer Chase were both attacked by fighters but returned safely. The Way crew also, once again, found themselves on the wrong end of a Nachtjäger's fury. Homeward bound, the Lancaster was still some two hours' flying time from Elsham when Zingelmann, ever alert, glimpsed what he took to be a Messerschmitt Bf210 some 900 yards away on the starboard quarter. He waited until the heavy fighter had closed to 600 yards before calling for a 'corkscrew', at which point the rear gunner opened fire. The Messerschmitt broke away and set off to look for easier prey, while the crew flew on into the night. They eventually landed without further incident at 0122 hours.

The squadron operated next on the night of 30/31 March, taking part in the dreadful slaughter over Nuremberg in which the RAF lost almost 100 aircraft in the space of only a few hours. No. 103 Squadron lost two crews, those of Flying Officer James Johnston and Pilot Officer Robert Tate. The Way crew was not operating that night, and was next on the Battle Order on 10 April, just at the time that the might of

Bomber Command was being redirected on to tactical targets specifically to support the invasion of Europe.

The target was Aulnoye, one of several railway yards identified for special attention. Twelve aircraft from No. 103 Squadron contributed to a total attacking force of thirty-two Lancasters and fifteen Pathfinder Mosquitoes. The raid was a success, with a good many locomotives put out of action – but it came at a cost. Several crews reported fighter activity and seven aircraft overall were shot down, including the crew of Pilot Officer John Armstrong, RNZAF, from Elsham Wolds.

Bill Way was luckier. Almost immediately after dropping its 14,000lb bombload, Lancaster ME722 was attacked by a Junkers Ju88, the enemy closing from dead astern. Both gunners – the established team of Jones and Zingelmann – opened fire, the pilot once again throwing the heavy bomber into a 'corkscrew'. Unusually another Lancaster flying close by witnessed the combat and also opened fire just as the enemy aircraft broke away.

Over the course of the next few weeks, the pace of operations accelerated and the targets varied. The Way crew flew seven further sorties in April to Rouen (18 April), Cologne (20 April), Düsseldorf (22 April), Karlsruhe (24 April), Friedrichshafen (27 April) and Maintenon (30 April).

The raid on Düsseldorf resulted in the deaths of Pilot Officer Thomas Astbury and his crew, who flew into the side of a hill on returning to base, and the 'failed to return' of Flying Officer J. W. Birchall and his crew, who would all later turn up as prisoners of war. The attack on Karlsruhe was also noteworthy, for several reasons.

The Lancaster of Flying Officer Thomas Leggett was hit by incendiaries from another aircraft and almost immediately became uncontrollable. The captain told his crew to prepare to abandon the plane, at which point the mid-upper gunner either left or was catapulted from his seat into the open sky. Leggett, however, managed to regain control of the Lancaster and fly home.

The Lancaster of Flight Sergeant Cecil Ogden was attacked by two Ju88s over the target and the gunners claimed to have shot one of them down and forced the other away, but only after their own aircraft was hit and seriously damaged. The captain made

Left
The air bomber,
John Gallacher, one
of the three officers
in the crew.
Anonymous

Right
Joseph Duns joined
the Way crew in
the rear turret for
their final flight.
Anonymous

for the emergency landing field at Manston with its extra long runway but was obliged to ditch in the Channel, the aircraft sinking in less than a minute. Remarkably, sixty seconds was sufficient time for all of the crew to make it out in one piece, and all were picked up safely by a local lifeboat.

Bill Way's Lancaster, ME722, which had been in the wars previously, was this time hit by flak over the target area but the crew and the aircraft made it home otherwise unscathed.

Two more crews were lost over Essen (Pilot Officer Frank Shepherd) and Friedrichshafen (Flight Lieutenant Maurice Cox, AFC – a pre-war regular airman) to bring a busy month to a close. But worse was to follow.

The raid on Mailly-le-Camp on 3/4 May is known to virtually every student of Bomber Command history as being one of the most disastrous of the war – not in terms of the destruction caused to the target, but rather to the attacking force who fell foul of a series of fatal mishaps. No. 103 Squadron put up fourteen aircraft, and all – including Lancaster ME722 with Bill Way at the controls – got away safely, taking a route via Reading and Beachy Head to the target in central France. Mailly was an established military base with troops and armour in abundance and an attractive target.

Way arrived over the target at 0026, having first had to orbit the assembly point, awaiting an instruction to bomb. The order seemed late in coming, problems with transmissions primarily to blame. With bomb doors closed and the aircraft relieved of its all heavy explosive (HE) load, Way headed for home. But behind him a number of No. 103 Squadron crews were fighting for their lives. And losing.

Squadron Leader Jock Swanston, Pilot Officer John Holden and an Australian Pilot Officer Sydney Rowe were all shot down, and Flying Officer Eric Broadbent was lucky to make it home after successfully fending off a determined fighter attack. Two other crews were obliged to land away from base. It was a poor night for the squadron, with a great many

empty seats at the post-op interrogation. It was a wretched night too for Bomber Command, which lost some forty-two aircraft in all. A tragedy that could and arguably should have been avoided.

But the squadron was not allowed long to lick its wounds. The aerodrome at Rennes St Jacques was the target for a badly executed attack on the night of 7/8 May, even though the squadron's Operations Record Book (ORB) suggests differently. There was one early return. A comparatively 'safe' minelaying trip (known as a 'gardening' sortie with the mines known as 'vegetables') took place on 10/11 May with little or no opposition encountered.

The Way crew was itself an early return on the raid to the Hasselt marshalling yards on 11/12 May as the result of a faulty compass. It was a disappointing trip all round for the squadron, with a number of the

Left Wireless operator Roger Cooper and navigator Derrick Hollingsworth. Friends in life, united in death.
Anonymous

crews being obliged to bomb targets of the last resort and two aircraft missing. One of those was piloted by a South African, Wing Commander Hubert Goodman, who had assumed command of the squadron only a few days before and who had already impressed the men with his press-on approach.

Two more minelaying sorties took place over Kiel Bay (15 May) and Aalborg (23 May), the former being yet another frustrating affair that led to two of the crews being obliged to return home with the 'vegetables' still in the bomb bay, and another of the aircraft shot down. Pilot Officer Kenneth Mitchell and his crew were all killed.

The railway marshalling yards in the historic city of Aachen were subject to two raids on 24/25 and 27/28 May. The former, a large attack comprising more than 400 aircraft, did less damage than the raid that followed two nights later by a force less than half the size. No. 103 Squadron put up 13 aircraft for the first and 12 for the second, the precise targets being the west marshalling yards and the Rothe Erde yards. The Way crew took part in both attacks without incident, despite many fighters being reported. Three aircraft were lost by the squadron over the two nights, that of Flight Sergeant Tate, Squadron Leader Ollier, DFC, AFM, and Flight Lieutenant Leggett.

As May turned to June, and the Supreme Allied Commander and his staff put the finishing touches to their invasion plans, the pace of operations and the range of targets increased significantly. The major showpiece battles, however, gave way to multiple, tactical raids involving smaller numbers of aircraft on precision targets: ammunition dumps; rail and road infrastructure; radar stations; and coastal gun batteries. But the attacks did not only take place in the proposed invasion area of Normandy; critically it was important to deceive the Germans into thinking that Calais was still the preferred landing ground, and targets were chosen accordingly.

On 2 June, No. 103 Squadron prepared fourteen aircraft for the short hop across the Channel and an attack on a series of gun positions in northern France. The weather was poor, both on take-off and over the target, with the crews struggling to see anything meaningful through the 10/10ths gloom. They had been instructed that if they could not see the markers, they were not to bomb.

Way had a distinguished guest on board for this particular flight, none other than the new officer commanding, Wing Commander John St John, DFC and bar, who had been posted to Elsham Wolds from 1656 Conversion Unit on 12 May. St John had won his two DFCs with 101 Squadron, the first for bringing a seriously damaged aircraft safely home. He would later add the DSO to his list of decorations, having completed three tours of operations.

History does not record whether St John was happy with what he saw; in the event, three of the squadron's crews brought their bombs back, and Way was one of eleven who completed the operation satisfactorily.

Yet another gun emplacement was singled out for an attack twenty-four hours later, this time in

Wimereux. The take-off was once again characterised by the unusually wet summer weather, but all fourteen squadron aircraft managed to get away on time, and all eventually returned to the UK having successfully bombed the target.

The relentless bombing of tactical targets in northern France continued; gun positions in Crisbecq were chosen for attention on the night of 5/6 June. The raid was unremarkable, save for the return flight when many of the crews reported seeing large numbers of ships in the Channel. The more astute among the crews realised at once that this was the invasion fleet, their suspicions confirmed not long after their return.

The Way crew was fast coming to the end of its first operational tour. They had flown eight operations in May, and were on the Battle Order on 6/7 June for their third operation for the month. At that rate they could expect to have finished their tour within weeks – an exciting prospect. But they were not complacent. The odds of survival typically improved in direct correlation to the experience gained, but the fickle hand of fate could strike at any time. And fate was unkind to Bill Way and his men.

Vire was the target. Way was once again in the pilot's seat with his 'regular' crew: Jennings; Gallacher; Hollingsworth; Cooper; and Zingelmann. The rear gunner was a 'spare'. Indeed, throughout their tour, the crew had flown with a variety of different air gunners in the tail, including most recently Bill Donnahey, who completed his second tour on the night of 2/3 June. On 3/4 June they had flown with Sergeant Hunt; over Crisbecq they had taken to the air with Flight Sergeant Wollard; for their final sortie, a nineteen-year-old Canadian – Flight Sergeant Joseph Duns – took the rear turret. Officially, Duns was on the strength of No. 576 Squadron, who were also at Elsham Wolds.

At the briefing, the crews were told they would be attacking two bridges that formed a vital link across the River Vire, and which could be used to rush German reinforcements towards the invasion area. No trip was ever without its risks, but operations to France were generally faced with less fear and trepidation than a long haul to Berlin or Stettin in the east, where the enemy was not only the Germans but also the weather, and the reliability of your aircraft.

The flight out was uneventful – all of the squadron's

eighteen aircraft getting away safely – with Flight Lieutenant Way – in Lancaster NE173 – leaving the ground at 2140 hours. Assembling over Base, the Lancasters headed for their first rendezvous point over Cheltenham and then on to Bridport before making for the Channel Islands and a straight run in to the target.

The raid was very much going according to plan. Despite heavy cloud, the Pathfinder Mosquitoes were still able to mark the target, some of the aircraft coming down as low as 3,000 feet to ensure the accuracy of their bombs. But flak and fighters were very much in evidence. Short of the target, Pilot Officer Frederick Knight of No. 460 Squadron was the first victim of the attack, the Australian's aircraft seen to explode in mid-air, showering debris in a wide arc over the French countryside. Then a second aircraft was observed going down, that of Canadian Flying Officer G. E. J. Bain from No. 576 Squadron, who had the misfortune of being stalked by Hauptmann Paul-Hubert Rauh. Now Rauh was looking for more 'trade' and, soon after, Lancaster NE173 was in his sights.

What happened next cannot be known with any certainty. Lancaster NE173 was seen to be hit and catch fire, but carried on flying. It then made a slow, descending turn 180 degrees to port, flying against the stream. Steadily the plane began to lose height, the aircrew choosing – or perhaps being obliged – to stay with their aircraft. When the Lancaster finally hit the ground it did so at a shallow angle that broke off the tail, while the main section continued to speed along the ground, shedding burning wreckage, before finally coming to rest a few yards short of a remote farmhouse.

Perhaps Bill had been attempting to crash-land. Perhaps he had dead or wounded on board. Maybe he was himself wounded, and unable to give the command to leave the aircraft. No one can possibly know. Whether by necessity or design, what is certain is that the crew stayed together until the very end, and died together as a result.

All seven were taken from the aircraft the next day and buried close to where they had fallen. They were later reinterred in three separate cemeteries: Bretteville-sur-Laize Canadian War Cemetery; Bény-sur-Mer Canadian War Cemetery; and the Bayeux War Cemetery. ●

CHAPTER SIX

UNLUCKY FOR SOME

BY HOWARD SANDALL

SIXTY-FOUR YEARS HAD PASSED SINCE FLIGHT SERGEANT JACK TREND'S LANCASTER PLUNGED INTO THE GROUND IN FLAMES. JACK RETURNED TO THE SMALL VILLAGE OF MEERLO IN HOLLAND TO BE GUEST OF HONOUR AT THE UNVEILING OF A MEMORIAL TO NO. 15 SQUADRON LANCASTER LM465, LS-U. IT WAS A SAD AND POIGNANT OCCASION FOR JACK; HE WAS THERE TO REMEMBER HIS SIX CREWMATES WHO PERISHED ON THAT FATEFUL NIGHT OF 13 JUNE 1944.

THE SOUND OF the skylark's song resonated across the airfield on a summer afternoon in Suffolk, England. Flight Sergeant Jack Trend sat at the edge of the airfield watching the activity from the ground crew making the four-engined Lancaster bombers ready for the night's operation. In the distance he could see small children messing about around the perimeter hoping to catch a glimpse of a Lancaster on a test flight. At twenty-one years old it had been just a few years earlier that Jack had taken part in a similar pastime. He sat for a while, briefly reminiscing about the innocence of that activity compared to what was expected of him as a wireless operator in Bomber Command. How times had changed and he felt anger towards the enemy for taking away his youth prematurely.

Jack's journey with Bomber Command commenced in October 1941 while he was serving in the Air Training Corps. He volunteered for aircrew instruction, and after the initial aptitude tests at Euston House in London he was graded as suitable for training as a wireless operator. On 1 January 1942 Jack arrived at RAF Padgate in Lancashire for his initial training, quickly followed a few weeks later by a posting to No. 2 Signals School in Blackpool for an intensive ground course. The next few months involved learning the basics of Morse code and gaining an understanding of the radio sets used by the RAF. Early 1943 brought a further posting to the Radio School at Yatesbury in Wiltshire where he experienced his first flight training in de Havilland Dominie and Percival Proctor aircraft. Aircrew needed to multitask and Jack was posted to No. 1 Air Armaments School at RAF Manby in Lincolnshire for a two-week ground gunnery course. In June 1943 Jack was posted to No. 3 Advanced Observer Flying School for intensive instruction in wireless operation and air gunnery, flying in the Avro Anson trainer.

After what seemed like an eternity, Jack was

classified as a competent wireless operator/air gunner. In August 1943 he was posted to No. 82 Operational Training Unit at RAF Ossington in Nottinghamshire. It was there that he 'crewed up' with four other airmen, including Carl Thompson, an American pilot, who was refused entry into the USAAF due to a leg deformity. Not deterred, Thompson crossed the border into Canada and joined the RCAF, where he was accepted for pilot training. Vickers Wellington bombers that had seen considerable operational service earlier in the war were now flying at No. 82 OTU. They were consequently war-weary machines and the reliability rate of the aircraft was poor to say the least. It was here that the crew learned to operate as a team, each one of them dependent on each other to fulfil their roles within the plane. The crew undertook cross-country bombing, navigational flights and the obligatory 'circuits and bumps' designed to assist the pilot to familarise himself with a twin-engined bomber. In early November 1943 the crew was posted to No. 1651 Conversion Unit at RAF Waterbeach and RAF Wratting Common for the next stage of their training. Flying in the four-engined Short Stirling required an additional two crew members. Tom Stubbs and Duke Pelham joined the team as mid-upper gunner and flight engineer respectively.

Operating as a crew of seven, Carl Thompson soon mastered the idiosyncrasies of the Stirling; perhaps the most difficult element was landing the aircraft with such a poor undercarriage configuration. Heavy landings sometimes caused the undercarriage to collapse, with the inevitable results.

On 27 December 1943 the crew undertook the final stage of their training. They arrived at No. 3 Lancaster Finishing School at RAF Feltwell for conversion on to the bomber they would take to war. Compared to the Stirling, the Avro Lancaster was a dream to fly and all the airmen became accustomed to the instruments and apparatus in double-quick time. A mixture of cross-country navigational and

Left Sergeant Jack Trend on completion of his air gunnery course in 1943. *Courtesy of J. Trend*

bombing exercises honed the crew's skills. Seven days later, on 2 January 1944, they finally arrived at RAF Mildenhall in Suffolk as part of 3 Group Bomber Command. No. 15 Squadron, to which the crew were being posted, was a pre-war squadron steeped in history and Jack felt very proud to be joining such an accomplished unit.

Their arrival at Mildenhall coincided with the squadron converting from the Short Stirling to the Avro Lancaster. The early part of the month consisted of lectures on survival and escape and evasion, something at the time Jack did not realise would become very relevant to his cause. As an entirely non-commissioned crew they were assigned a small terraced house within the central confines of the camp, although they took their meals in the sergeants' mess. The crew members that arrived for operational duties at Mildenhall consisted of the following:

Pilot: Flight Sergeant Carlton Stewart Thompson, RCAF, from Michigan, USA;
Navigator: Sergeant Roderick McMillan, RCAF, from Victoria, British Columbia;
Bomb aimer: Sergeant Ronald George Lemky, RCAF, from Saskatoon;
Wireless operator: Sergeant Jack M. Trend, RAF, from Brighton in Sussex;
Mid-upper gunner: Sergeant Thomas Edward Stubbs, RAF, from Brockley in London;
Rear gunner: Sergeant Richard Sidney Mobbs, RAF, from Cratfield in Suffolk;
Flight engineer: Sergeant Maurice Bernard Pelham, RAF, from Stamford Hill in London.

In early 1944 Bomber Command's strategic bombing of Germany's industrial cities continued at a pace. Historians consider the period from November 1943

Right No. 1651 Conversion Unit course, November –December 1943. Members of aircrew destined for either Nos. 15 or 622 Squadrons pose for a course photograph. Jack Trend's crew are standing second row from back, L–R: second from left, Sergeant Lemky, Sergeant Trend, Sergeant Stubbs; second row from front seated: immediate left, Sergeant Thompson, Sergeant McMillan.
Courtesy of J. Trend

to March 1944 attributable to the Battle of Berlin. The weather towards the end of January improved, and Jack and the crew found themselves on the Battle Order for their first mission to bomb the industrial heart of Augsburg as part of 594 bombers dispatched. Several missions occurred in quick succession to heavily defended targets in the Ruhr Valley, including two trips to Stuttgart in early March and two to Frankfurt on the 18th and 22nd. Berlin was the target on 24 March and the final mission to the city during the Battle of Berlin. The operation was severely hampered by strong winds blowing the aircraft off course every step of the way. The bomber stream became very scattered and several planes ventured over heavily defended areas en route to the target and back. Commissioned in the rank of pilot officer the previous day, Carl Thompson was struggling to keep on course and overshot the target area. There was no

alternative but to circle around and join the bomber stream again, an extremely dangerous undertaking with the risk of collision high and another opportunity for the German defences to pick up the bomber. Over the target the bomb aimer was unable to see the target indicators and therefore released the bombs on the fires burning below. Holding the Lancaster steady over the target to obtain the obligatory photograph seemed like an age to the crew, who were being buffeted intensely by the flak defences. Sergeant Lemky confirmed that the photo had been taken and Pilot Officer Thompson threw the bomber into a steep dive to clear the target area swiftly. No sooner had the aircraft levelled out than they were attacked by a night fighter that sprayed cannon shells into the fuselage, damaging the ammunition ducts and rear elevator trim cables. Luckily LM465 avoided any further major damage and returned to Mildenhall

safely. Seventy-two bombers from the main force did not return to base.

This particular period for Bomber Command was not successful and the German night-fighter force reaped revenge on the bomber crews, inflicting heavy losses. Berlin was at the outer limits for the aircraft deployed, and a combination of weather conditions and improved night-fighter techniques meant that the attrition rates could not be sustained indefinitely.

Fortunately for the crew, April 1944 brought a new strategic direction for Bomber Command, with the focus switching to support for the Allied invasion. However, excursions into the Ruhr were still being detailed, interspersed among the French and Belgium invasion support targets. During April and May Pilot Officer Thompson and his crew completed seventeen sorties to various industrial city objectives including Aachen, Cologne, Düsseldorf, Karlsruhe, Essen, Friedrichshafen, Duisburg and Dortmund. Targets in support of the impending invasion embraced Rouen, Cap Gris-Nez and Courtrai in France.

The prelude to D-Day began on the morning of 5 June, although due to the secrecy of the invasion Jack and his crew thought it was just another operation. At 0800 hours the adjutant's parade occurred and the afternoon was taken up with two squadrons

air testing their Lancasters. This usually involved a flight of twenty-five minutes to check navigational aids, guns, radio, electrics and the hydraulic system. Any faults were reported to the ground crew and the committed staff would set to work immediately to rectify any identified faults.

Jack describes the build-up to the operation:

The briefing that day took place very late in the evening, we had a separate briefing to that of 622 Squadron who shared Mildenhall with us. As soon as the operational target was revealed all the aircraft were bombed up with 11 x 1,000Ib

bombs and 3 x 500Ib high explosive bombs. In addition the ground crews put in 1,516 gallons of fuel. The meteorology officer delivered his forecast as extremely cloudy with some drizzle. Our target was to be the German 105mm gun emplacements situated between the Caen canal and the River Orme at Ouistreham. We later found out that it was essential to destroy the target to allow the first wave of troops onto the beaches.

With all the pre-flight checks made and our equipment collected, we were driven out to the dispersal point in darkness of the early hours of 6th June. The vital engine warm up began and at 0345 hours, we left the runway behind and climbed to 6,500 feet following a course over Rochester, then Hastings. From here we set out across the English Channel towards Ouistreham on the Normandy coast. The run in to the target was timed for 0500hrs. The cloud that night was up to 12,000 feet and we could clearly see the Pathfinder Mosquitoes accompanying us. There was little if any Luftwaffe activity, but anti-aircraft fire and rocket salvos were considerable as we approached the target area. After our bombs had been released, it was a quick turn round before we headed back to Mildenhall to complete our E.T.A. at 0700 hours.

Before we arrived back at base, I received a B.B.C. announcement on the aircraft wireless as the breaking news about the D-Day invasion was being transmitted all over the country. The bombing offensive that we'd taken part in, had been the start of the Allied landings in France. My heart began to beat somewhat faster as I relayed this exciting but not unexpected news to the captain and the rest of the crew via the intercommunication system. For the remainder of the journey we were in an upbeat mood.

Left Navigational chart for the D-Day operation to bomb the Normandy coastal batteries, prepared by Flying Officer R.L. Urwin, DFM, the navigator in the crew of Flight Lieutenant Hargreaves, DFC, from No. 622 Squadron. *Courtesy of J. Urwin*

We landed safely and after the routine de-briefing we retired to bed emotionally exhausted by our efforts. We were roused for lunch and informed that we would be operating again that same night. The target was announced at a joint briefing for 15 and 622 Squadrons because we would be attacking the same target. Our objective was to bomb specific military targets in Lisieux, the biggest town after Caen in the invasion area. Weather conditions were reported to be improving in the area, therefore at 2340 hours thirty-three bombers took off for a return to the Normandy coast. As we approached the target we bombed on the red marker left by the Mosquito Pathfinders, which were accurately placed. Our arrival above Lisieux coincided with a break in the clouds and we could see the town clearly laid out below. Once again there was little Luftwaffe activity and sporadic anti-aircraft fire.

We landed at Mildenhall for a second time that day at 0300 hours, whereupon we were de-briefed and then thanked our lucky stars for having survived such a memorable day. Every single aircraft belonging to 15 and 622 Squadrons had fulfilled their missions that day and returned home safely.

Just six nights later, on 12 June 1944, the briefing room in the Operations complex at RAF Mildenhall was full to its capacity. Some of the assembled 150 aircrew belonging to Nos. 15 and 622 Squadrons had to stand at the side or at the back. The usual simmering, rum-bling undertone of conversation was evident as the anticipation increased. It stopped in an instant; the two squadrons' commanding officers entered the room, immediately receiving the attention of the massed audience. Wing Commander Watkins, DSO, DFC, DFM, moved quickly to the front and up the few steps to the stage.

The instant coming to attention was not just a re-action of accepted compliance to military tradition, but of genuine regard for the respective squadron commanders. The majority of the aircrew were non-commissioned officers (sergeants and flight sergeants) in those days and they knew their commanders had experienced operations. Wing Commander Watkins was well respected among the crews. His Distinguished Flying Medal proved his courage and outstanding ability, which had been officially recognised when he also had been a sergeant – one of them!

Watkins motioned for his crews to be seated and when the shuffling had settled the high curtains parted to reveal large maps of East Anglia to southern Europe. There were some quiet gasps of disparagement, even quieter short whistles, and from some just the word 'Jesus' passed their lips.

Watkins spoke: 'Gentlemen, the target for tonight is Gelsenkirchen, once again. We have bombed this

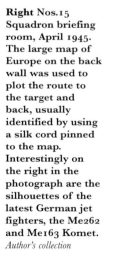

Right Nos.15 Squadron briefing room, April 1945. The large map of Europe on the back wall was used to plot the route to the target and back, usually identified by using a silk cord pinned to the map. Interestingly on the right in the photograph are the silhouettes of the latest German jet fighters, the Me262 and Me163 Komet. *Author's collection*

industrial enemy giant before, but its importance in the production of oil is already well known. Intelligence has it that in spite of previous bombing by us and the USAAF, production has not been materially reduced. It is indeed a committed German industrial city. A force of up to 300 Bomber Command aircraft will strike it tonight. As some of us know already, targets in this area of Germany are notoriously well defended and the mission will not be easy, no bombing mission ever is! The Luftwaffe will be our major concern as well as other bombers in such a large force. Extra care and vigilance will be necessary, even more so than usual. Good luck!'

The wing commander motioned with a partially raised finger and in a soft voice he asked the squadron leader to step on to the stage. The station intelligence officer came forward, the first of the specialist officers, several of whom sat in the front row of easy chairs. Other leaders, flight commanders, navigation officer, engineering, signals, armament, and gunnery leader, would follow. Station padres were always asked to be present and took a passive role. The presentation lasted on average thirty to forty minutes and there was always a short applause when the catering officer announced that chocolate and sweet rations should be collected from the officer nominated.

Finally, the noisy shuffling of chairs indicated the crews' departure to the locker clothing rooms to prepare for the night's flying and for final words from their specialist leaders. Then it was on to chat-up the young WAAFs who had packed the parachutes; they would hand over the parachute after a final check of the safety pin, this last piece of survival kit. Sergeant Jack Trend looked at his crew prior to leaving the briefing room and he realised that the initial doubts in each other's abilities had well and truly disappeared. This would be Jack's twenty-first mission and they had been assigned their usual aircraft, Lancaster LM465, LS-U. They were a proficient crew, professional once in the air and inseparable when on the ground. Their 'tour' to date had been relatively uneventful except for 30 April, when a violent swing forced their Lancaster off the runway, resulting in a ground loop and subsequent crash. Fortunately, all the crew walked away unhurt.

Warrant Officer McMillan, RCAF, and the other navigators now knew for the first time exactly the target and routes to be flown, not only to the objective,

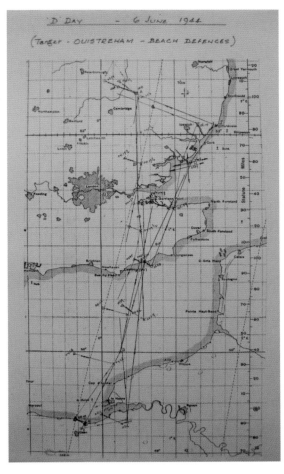

Left Navigational chart for the D-Day operation
Courtesy of J. Urwin

but also tracks to get back home. They would have to spend time on their charts and maps. Crews would subsequently be taken to the aircraft dispersals – often quite a distance away – in either aircrew coaches but more often in three-ton trucks. Each in turn proceeded with their parachute in hand to have a quick word with their ground crews. The pilot and senior flight sergeant (chiefy) or warrant officer engineer would spend time discussing the engine servicing and airframe etc, with a final outside scrutiny and inspection of the bombload. The closing of the huge bomb doors were one of the last checks when all four Merlin engines were running, before accepting the aircraft's airworthiness state and signing the special RAF document known as form 700.

Navigators usually needed help with all the 'clobber' they had to carry in addition to a parachute: there was a large case with maps, rulers, computing aids and manuals, sometimes even a larger canvas bag and a heavy Plexiglas case containing his semi-

Right Lancaster LM465, LS-U stands on the dispersal point in April 1944. The discerning eye will notice the racks of incendiary bombs waiting to be loaded into the bomb bay. *Courtesy of J. Trend*

automated sextant. There was always an opportunity for a quick visit to the bathroom before jumping on the transport to the dispersal, as there were no such facilities on the windswept isolated dispersals far from anywhere. The next chance might be as much as ten or twelve hours later, unless the brave used the Elsan toilet on board.

At approximately 2315 hours Pilot Officer Carl Thompson lifted LM465, LS-U off the runway at RAF Mildenhall, along with fourteen other Lancasters from No. 15 Squadron and seventeen from No. 622 Squadron. The bombers climbed towards the rendezvous point over Southwold on the Suffolk coast. The German radar controllers were already plotting the aircrafts' estimated course and target. The only question for the controllers was what the actual objective was. Diversionary and spoof raids made it difficult for the German plotters to instruct the night fighters to join the bomber stream at a particular point.

Carl Thompson settled into keeping the Lancaster on a precise course heading as directed by Warrant Officer McMillan, RCAF, in the navigator's spot. The crew crossed the Dutch coast at 0053 hours on schedule and expected that the German night-fighter force would have picked up the bomber stream some time ago and were planning their interception.

Silhouetted against the night sky, Unteroffizier Gustav Sarzio from 6 Gruppe/Nachtjagdgeschwader 1, manoeuvred his Me110G night fighter stealthily underneath the British bomber. Rear gunner Sergeant Richard (Dick) Mobbs peered endlessly into the night sky, oblivious to the danger creeping ever closer below. Sarzio positioned his Schrage Musik gun configuration to fire in between the engines on the wing in an attempt to give the crew time to bail out. Approximately twenty kilometres north-west of Venlo, in the province of Limburg, he fired his 20mm cannon shells into the bomber's starboard inner engine and fuselage, instantly setting the wing alight in a mass of flames. Carl Thompson fought with the controls knowing that the bomber was now doomed to go down. With no alternative he ordered the crew to bail out.

Jack Trend recalls his account of the night:

I was listening to the Group broadcast at 0100 hours when we appeared to be hit by cannon shells, the starboard inner engine was on fire with a second fire near the SBA equipment, amidships. Our pilot Carl Thompson was giving instructions to bail out and I followed the bomb aimer Ron Lemky and Duke Pelham out of the forward hatch. I observed what I thought was a river just before landing, this turned out to be a road when I tried to dump my parachute. I eventually buried it on the other side of the road. I heard the sound of what must have been clogs on tarmac, I didn't know that a curfew was in force and realized that these people must have been looking for me. I crossed the road again when all was quiet and hid in a corn field until mid-afternoon. From my hiding spot I heard and saw Germans with dogs searching the area but I stayed hidden. I thought that there was a built up area on the east side of the field possibly electrical installations or water plant. I had previously checked that I was all in one piece, just a minor nosebleed and a burning sensation on my face. I moved out onto the main road, thankful to be able to stretch my legs, into the sun and walked south.

Holland was alongside the main route utilised by Bomber Command to deliver its deadly cargo. The intensity of the German night-fighter force in 1944 resulted in many aircrew being shot down and on the run behind enemy lines in the Dutch countryside. For each and every one of them the mercy and courage shown by the local people was beyond measure. Holland as a country is flat, open terrain criss-crossed by a labyrinth of dykes and waterways. Evaders found themselves trying to cross a river when the only way was over a guarded bridge. All the obstacles meant that escaping out of Holland was very difficult indeed. The Dutch population was very sympathetic to aircrew, but anyone found assisting or harbouring airmen would face the penalty of torture, prison camp or even death.

After walking a little way Jack came across a farmer and, by gesturing, made him understand his plight; fortunately he was pointed in the right direction. On the outskirts of town (now known as Meerlo), Jack

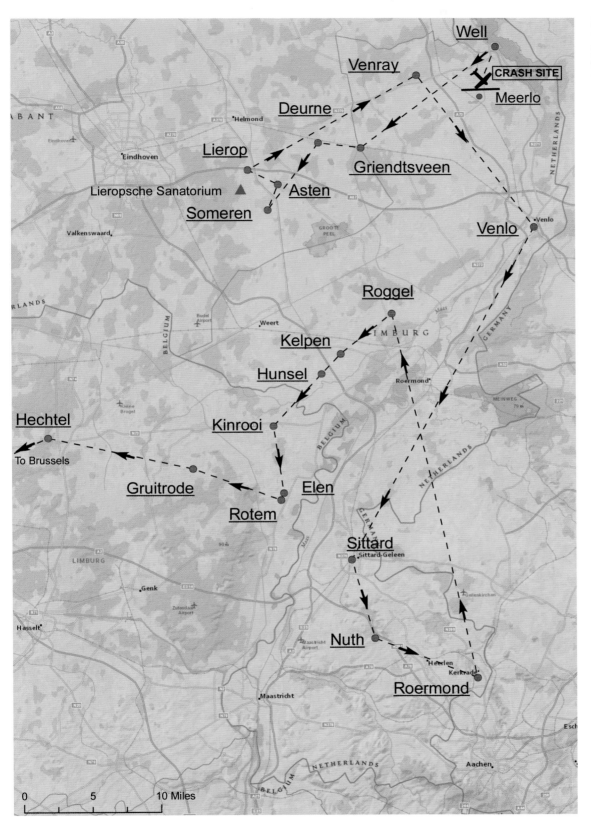

Left Map of crash site and evasion route taken by Jack Trend across Holland and Belgium. *Courtesy of Mariska and Hans Van Dam*

Well

Venray

CRASH SITE

Meerlo

Deurne

Lierop

Griendtsveen

Lieropsche Sanatorium

Asten

Someren

Venlo

Roggel

Kelpen

Hunsel

Hechtel

Kinrooi

To Brussels

Gruitrode

Elen

Rotem

Sittard

Nuth

Roermond

0   5   10 Miles

came across a farmhouse where he was given shelter. The farmer and his two daughters provided a meal for him and gave him civilian clothes in exchange for his revolver. The danger of discovery was ever present, therefore Jack rested in the chicken house. At 2130 hours he was introduced to a guide who took him over the River Maas by bicycle to the house of the burgomaster in Well. After some questioning to determine his identity, he slept the night at 'Pop' Krebbers's house.

The morning of 14 June dawned bright and Jack recalled that it was his twenty-second birthday. But

Right A poor copy of the new identity given to Jack Trend by his Dutch helpers. *Courtesy of J. Trend*

any celebrations would have to be put on hold, for he was required to cycle with Pop Krebbers for a distance of 30km to Griendtsveen where he met other members of the Dutch resistance movement. He was surprised to receive a birthday cake, a tot of whisky and some cigarettes. The kindness shown by his helpers was brought to an abrupt end when he was asked to sleep in the garden shed.

It was around this time that news of the other crew members reached Jack. Centrally between the churches at Meerlo and Tienray six aircrew bodies had been found near a crashed Lancaster. The Germans buried them in separate coffins in the local churchyard at Venlo. The airmen were found lying next to both open and unopened parachutes. Jack was extremely disturbed to hear the news and surmised that the bomber exploded soon after he exited, killing his crewmates.

On 15 June Jack was allowed to listen to BBC radio and also received his forged identity card. He was now Johann Pieters, a deaf and dumb pianist. A few more days passed and Jack was introduced to a Polish evader; together they cycled to Lierop via Deurne-Someran and Asten. At 2345 hours he arrived at camp 'Denne Lust/Stroubouw' also known as the 'Sanitorium' where he met other escapees, namely a Canadian called Bob Punter and Eric Grisdale, a RAF pilot, both part of the same No. 626 Squadron

crew. The days passed slowly at the camp and the evaders occupied themselves by playing cards and teaching the young Dutchmen (Onderduikers) the Morse code in exchange for lessons in the Dutch language. The highlight of the day was the arrival of the daily meal, which usually comprised a mixture of sandwiches, potatoes and fruit.

Camp Denne Lust was built in reaction to the challenges faced by evaders after the Normandy landings on 6 June. The Allied aircraft were striking targets of opportunity at will, especially railways, bridges and supply routes. The Germans were retreating in the face of the Allied onslaught and the 'safe' houses used by the Dutch Resistance were now being overrun on a frequent basis. The solution came in the form of hastily built camps in wooded areas that could not be attributed to any one, or group, of resistance members. One such camp was Denne Lust or Zwarte Park. Jack remembers his first sight of the camp: 'Coming off the side roads we came to the usual fire tracks which split up this section of pine forest. We dismounted from our bicycles and walked into the wood up until we reached a clearing. There were a number of small straw houses built into the trees. In the distance I could see the offices and a large pit was obscured some way away.'

Towards the end of June more evaders, namely Eddy Walker (RAF), Harry Cooper and Bill Kinney (both USAAF), joined the group. At around mid-morning on 8 July, Jack and the others left the camp by car. The journey took them to Crisis Hoeve where they were sheltered. The following day the journey continued by train to Venray and then on to Sittard, where Jack parted company with the others . He was destined for Nuth with two other aircrew to be housed at Mr Pinckaer's in the Stationstrasse. The days passed uneventfully until 20 July when three additional evaders arrived. While at Nuth, Jack was presented with his new 'carte identite'; he was now Rene Joseph Colin, a coal miner at 'Jemeppe'.

The passage of time was excruciatingly slow and to Jack every day brought more anxiety about being discovered. He was desperate to get home and wondered if his mother had received the dreaded letter from the commanding officer informing her that he was missing in action, presumed dead. After a thorough briefing by his helpers, Jack and the others left

Nuth by train, destined for Roermond. Fortunately his false documents passed the check points and he settled into his seat on the train and hid behind a newspaper. On arrival the entire group cycled across Maas Bridge, straight past a sentry who just let them pass. The journey initially continued by car on 29 July and then by boat ride to a place known as the 'Shack' at Roggel, about one and a half miles outside the village. Twelve evaders in total arrived and they all slept in huts suitable for six people. The next few days passed without incident; however, every day brought more anxiety and impatience to get home. The morning of 12 August dawned and Jack and his comrades endured a car journey to Huntsvel orchard at Kelpen. The resistance movement had built a camp in the woods at Kinrooi just inside the Belgian border, and Jack and the others arrived there on 17 August. He slept in the open, but as the nights were getting colder all returned to the barn nearby for some warmth. One morning the whole party were woken early and warned about Germans approaching. They made a swift exit and escaped into the woods. The Germans suspected the barn may be hiding fugitives and blew it up with hand grenades.

On 1 September there was a further relocation, to Elen, another staging post on the route to freedom. Unbeknown to Jack at the time, extensive plans were made to avoid capture. It was evident that the Allied advance was close by and they all witnessed German troops retreating along the roads. A few days later the party was on the move again, arriving at Rotem where he resided with a group of partisans who cooked an entire sheep in a large pot. Jack tried to sleep under a tree but the rain and the cold, damp conditions kept him awake. Just before dawn four German troops routed the camp and they all ran for their lives; Jack jumped into a ditch to hide. Without realising, he dropped his identity card in the ditch. It was now unsafe to remain at the camp so the party took over the ticket collector's office at Rotem. The next day the entire group returned to where they were forced to flee from the German troops, which enabled Jack to find his identity card. It was clear that the area was now overrun by the retreating Germans, so on the night of 8 September the group left Rotem and walked until they were exhausted.

From a vantage point Jack spotted a vehicle with the American star on the side. Hopes were raised and

Left Evaders photographed while at Kinrooi camp in the woods. Back L–R: Eric Grisdale, Denis Walker, Robert Punter; Front L–R: Leslie Shimmins, Roger Gardiner, Jack Trend.
Courtesy of J. Trend

No.15 Squadron,
Royal Air Force,
MILDENHALL,
Suffolk.

13th June 1944.

Dear Mrs. Trend,

You will now have received my telegram stating that
your Son, 1397945 Flight Sergeant John Melville Trend, failed
to return from an operational flight on the night of 12/13th
June 1944. I am writing to express my deepest sympathy with
you in your anxiety, and also to encourage you to hope that
he is safe.

He was the Wireless Operator of an aircraft engaged
on an important bombing mission over enemy territory, and
after take-off nothing further was heard. It appears likely
that the aircraft was forced down, and if this is the case,
there is some chance that he may be safe, and a prisoner of
war.

In this event it may be two to three months before
any certain information is obtained through the International
Red Cross, but I hope the news will soon come through.

I should be grateful if you would inform me should
you receive a prisoner of war card from your Son. My reason
for making this request is that a Squadron Prisoner of War
Fund arranges a monthly despatch of comforts, and I am most
anxious to include your Son's name on the list at the
earliest possible moment.

It is desired to explain that the request in the
telegram notifying you of the casualty of your Son was
included with the object of avoiding his chance of escape
being prejudiced by undue publicity in case he was still at
large. This is not to say that any information about him is
available, but is a precaution adopted in the case of all
personnel reported missing.

Your Son had done excellent work in the Squadron, and
had successfully completed twenty operational flights. He will
be very much missed by his many friends in the Squadron.

His personal effects have been safeguarded and will
be dealt with by the Committee of Adjustment Officer, R.A.F.
Station, Mildenhall, as soon as possible, who will write to
you in the near future.

May I on behalf of the whole Squadron express to you
our most sincere sympathy, and the hope that you will soon
receive good news.

Yours sincerely,

Wing Commander.
(W. D.G. WATKINS. DFC. .DFM.)

while trekking along some tank tracks he came across an American advance party. The tension and anxiety endured over the last few days ebbed away. Safety and liberation on 11 September will always be significant for Jack. The whole group was driven to the Intelligence Corps headquarters at Guitrode, a RAF Canadian Unit emergency aerodrome (TAF Unit) where they were debriefed and enjoyed American hospitality. The morning of 14 September will live long in the memory for Jack. He was transferred to Brussels where he boarded a Dakota transport plane destined for England. They lifted off the runway at 1400 hours and touched down at RAF Hendon at 1700.

It was around midday on 16 September when Jack arrived back in Brighton. The realisation of what his mother had been through was etched on her face during an emotional reunion.

In 2008 Jack attended the unveiling of a memorial to his crew at the exact position the Lancaster crashed sixty-four years before. He was the guest of honour on the day, with local dignitaries, the local mayor, veterans and officials from the squadron also attending the event.

The main panel of the monument is made from a fragment of the metal skin of the Lancaster, with the inscription of the six crew members who lost their lives. As Jack stood alongside the memorial, images of his crew returned in a moment of emotional remembrance. His thoughts ventured to a reported scene that he has visualised in his mind many times over the passing years: a Lancaster bomber burns in the distance with six young airmen lying motionless near their parachutes, under the shadow of a church. For Jack's six friends in his crew, the night of 12/13 June was a tragedy and would have a lifetime effect on their families.

The passing years have not dulled Jack's memories and he takes solace from the fact that his crew will be remembered for posterity. This story of heroism and terrible misfortune was the norm for many Bomber Command crews. To a significant degree their lives depended on a twist of fate. Ask any member of Bomber Command how they survived a full tour of operations and the response will be a combination of teamwork and luck. For six members of the Thompson crew on that night in June 1944, their luck finally ran out. Unlucky for some! ●

Left Showing remarkable emotional restraint, Jack stands and reflects on the events that unfolded in June 1944. With the unveiling ceremony over and wreaths laid, the Meerlo brass band can play one last tribute to fallen heroes.
Courtesy of A. Wheatley

CHAPTER SEVEN

FOR HE'S A JOLLY GOOD FELLOW

BY SEAN FEAST

IN THE NO. 550 SQUADRON OPERATIONS RECORD BOOK (ORB), THE ENTRY FOR 16/17 JUNE 1944 CONCLUDES WITH THE FOLLOWING: 'IT IS REGRETTED THAT THREE OF OUR AIRCRAFT FAILED TO RETURN, NO NEWS BEING RECEIVED SINCE TAKE OFF: 'V' (SQUADRON LEADER SMITH DFC – 'B' FLIGHT COMMANDER); 'H' (FLYING OFFICER NEILSON) AND 'P' (PILOT OFFICER PACKHAM). AMONG THE CREW OF FLYING OFFICER NEILSON WAS THE SQUADRON BOMBING LEADER FLIGHT LIEUTENANT MCCONNELL DFC. THEY WILL BE SADLY MISSED, FOR THEY WERE ALL JOLLY GOOD FELLOWS'. GEOFF PACKHAM WAS ONE OF THOSE FELLOWS WHO FAILED TO RETURN.

GEOFF PACKHAM had only been with No. 550 Squadron for a little over a fortnight before he went missing on the night of 16/17 June 1944. But he was by no means an inexperienced pilot. Indeed, after almost three years of continual flying, he had amassed more than 800 hours to his name.

Born in Sheffield on 22 January 1922, Geoff was educated at the local grammar school and started work as an audit clerk in the Town Hall in 1938. His passion for flying was kindled by his father, who had been a fighter pilot in the First World War: 'My father was a lieutenant in the Royal Flying Corps [RFC] who was flying with No. 50 Squadron in the summer of 1918 in the defence of London. One evening on a night-time interception, his engine caught fire, and with no parachute he side-slipped the SE5 down to the ground as quickly as possible. When the aircraft hit he was catapulted out, striking the Lewis gun mount above him and rendering him unconscious. When help finally arrived and they found the cockpit empty, it took them some time to find him. He was badly injured and spent six months in hospital.' A further 'need for speed' was engendered by his uncle and aunt. His aunt in particular was a well-known motorcycle racer of the time who actively encouraged both Geoff and his younger brother Peter to compete.

Left Geoffrey Packham with his younger brother Peter, who was also destined to become a pilot.
Geoffrey Packham

Volunteering for aircrew service in the Royal Air Force at the end of 1940, Geoff's training followed the usually prescribed route, completing his Initial Training Wing at 3 ITW Torquay. His flying instruction took place in Canada, firstly at 31 Elementary Flying Training School (EFTS) in Calgary and De Winton, before progressing to 34 Service Flying Training School (SFTS) in Medicine Hat. He went solo (on 25 September 1941) in less than nine hours, and easily converted from single- to twin-engined training aircraft. At the conclusion of his initial

Left Geoff's father with his SE5, which he flew in the defence of London in 1918.
Geoffrey Packham

courses he was rated 'above average' – a reflection of his natural abilities at the controls of an aircraft.

Returning to the UK in March 1942, Geoff was posted to 12 Advanced Flying Unit (AFU) and might soon after have expected to proceed to an Operational Training Unit and a squadron, but instead found himself at a Heavy Glider Conversion Unit (HGCU) in Brize Norton towing Horsa gliders and teaching the Army pilots how to fly. For a man keen to get into the war, there was more frustration when he was posted to 7 Air Gunnery School (AGS) at Stormy Down: 'I was a bit cheesed off but someone in the Air Ministry clearly decided where people were needed and I was needed at Stormy Down. I spent exactly a year at 7 AGS, throwing a Whitley around in the skies while parties of trainee air gunners would try and shoot down an attacking fighter or fire at a target drogue.'

Again maintaining his 'above average' rating, it was not until November 1943 that he was rescued from AGS and posted to 18 OTU – shared between RAF Finningley and RAF Worksop – the final step in the journey towards an operational squadron. It was at OTU that he 'crewed up': 'I was late and by the time I arrived most of the crews had already formed. There was a group of sergeants, however, who were all together and looking for a pilot. Given that I had about 800 hours to my name at that time they seemed very happy to have me, and for my part I could not have wished for a better crew.'

Geoff enjoyed his time at OTU, even flying clapped-out Wellingtons that had seen better days and which occasionally refused to leave the ground. He enjoyed the sense of danger and thrived on it. He kept an old motorbike and, as Finningley was comparatively close to Sheffield, he was able to pop home whenever he could to see his parents. He could also hear how his brother was doing. 'Peter too had joined the RAF and was sent to Florida to learn how to fly. He was training to be a fighter pilot but burst his eardrums. Eventually he was posted out to the Far East flying DC3s.'

From 18 OTU the crew was transferred to RAF Lindholme, converting to four engines (in this case the Handley Page Halifax) at 1667 Heavy Conversion Unit (HCU) at neighbouring Sandtoft. They then spent a fortnight at No. 1 Lancashire Finishing School (1 LFS), learning the idiosyncrasies of the aircraft they would fly in anger, before finally arriving at No. 550 Squadron, North Killingholme.

No. 550 Squadron was a main-force squadron that had been formed in November 1943 at RAF Waltham and soon after moved to North Killingholme. It gloried under the motto *Per ignem vincimus* (Through fire we conquer). By the time Geoff and his crew arrived

at the end of May 1944, the squadron was on its second officer commanding, Wing Commander 'Pat' Connolly. (A regular officer and former fighter pilot, Connolly was killed less than two months later on an operation to Revigny.)

As was customary, Geoff's first 'op' was as a 'second dickey' to a more senior crew; as such Geoff found himself in the company of the 'B' Flight commander, Squadron Leader Gavin Smith, DFC, for what turned out to be a historic trip. The squadron pro-

squadron aircraft returned home without incident.

Having completed his first operation successfully, the very next night Geoff went with his own crew to Paris to bomb the rail junction at Achères. Thick cloud over the target obscured the aiming point and most of the squadron aircraft came home with their bombs still on board. One crew failed to return (Pilot Officer Tyrrell Shervington in Lancaster ME556. All on board were killed). A trip to Flers on the night of 9 June was followed by another attempt on Achères

Left Geoff's aunt was a well-known motorcycle racer in the 1930s.
Geoffrey Packham

vided eighteen aircraft for an attack on a coastal battery commanding a strategic position on the Cherbourg peninsula at Crisbecq. In the words of the squadron's ORB for 5 June: 'Although some cloud was encountered across England on the outward journey enough was seen to realise that the whole of southern England was on the move. Whilst flying across the Channel a vast armada, of ships, was seen making their way towards France.'

It was a No. 550 Squadron aircraft that was the first to bomb at 2334 hours, thus spearheading the attack for the invasion of Europe the following morning. Very little flak was encountered and all of the

on the 10th, this time with more result. Two further operations to Gelsenkirchen (12 June) and Le Havre (14 June) followed before Geoff and his crew were briefed for an attack on the synthetic oil facility at Sterkrade on the 16th. Detailed as part of an attacking force of 321 bombers and Pathfinder Mosquitoes, it was to be their seventh and final trip: 'I was given Squadron Leader Smith's old aircraft [LL 747, BQ-P 'Peter'] and he took a newer one. "Peter" was a little bit past her sell-by date (she had nearly 300 hours to her credit) as I was soon to find out, and although we had been instructed to bomb from 21,000ft, I couldn't get her to go anything above 18,000ft.'

Being unable to make a higher ceiling potentially exposed Geoff's Lancaster to more flak, and when twenty or so minutes' flying time from the target, it all started to go wrong: 'The bomb aimer Johnny Jenkins was getting ready in the nose when there was suddenly a terrific flash and a fire that quickly started but equally quickly went out, but it was clear that we had been hit. Flak had punched a hole in the fuselage and knocked out one of the engines (the port inner). A second engine (the port outer) was also faltering. As well as the engines and the fuselage, the Perspex in

Right Geoff as a young sergeant pilot. At the time he was rated 'above average'.
Geoffrey Packham

the nose had been shattered and some of the instruments were out of action, including the airspeed indicator, which made life difficult.'

Geoff increased the revs on the two remaining 'good' engines and assessed the damage. Mercifully, none of the crew had been injured, but the hydraulic systems had been rendered unserviceable, cutting power to the turrets. This meant that they were effectively defenceless should they be attacked by a night fighter. Geoff then tried to open the bomb doors:

We carried on to the target with every intention of bombing, but could not get the bomb doors to move, in spite of the efforts of the bomb aimer, navigator and flight engineer who were all working on the problem. We were by now over the target area, had lost more height and could well have been on our own now

in all the flak.

After two or three minutes I decided to abandon the mission and head towards the nearest point of the English coast. There was no way I could land without brakes or flaps, and with a full bombload on board, but I thought that if I could get close enough to home then the boys could bail out. It was going to be touch and go because we were still losing height. The second engine had by now given up, so I was flying with just the two starboard engines, which made trimming and control of the aircraft quite a problem.

About fifteen minutes after leaving the target area, a difficult situation suddenly became worse. A twin-engined Messerschmitt Bf110 was spotted on the starboard quarter. One of the gunners opened fire, but it was little more than a futile gesture since he could not traverse his guns. Geoff took evasive action as best he could and the fighter overshot, disappearing into the gloom from whence it came.

The Lancaster flew on, the two good engines straining in their mounts and running increasingly hot with the excess power now being demanded of them. Then another Messerschmitt (or possibly the same one) attacked, and again Geoff took evasive action, losing yet more height in the process. 'I knew now that we would never reach England and told the boys that we'd have to bail out. They were all remarkably calm as they made their way to the front of the aircraft. I remember there was some difficulty in opening the hatch but it gave way after some persuasion from the bomb aimer who lost his flying boot in the process.'

One by one the crew clipped on their parachutes and bailed out, the bomb aimer pausing only to gather his lucky teddy bear before jumping through the hatch and leaving his skipper alone at the controls. Geoff has little recollection of what happened next: 'I had to undo my straps, take off my helmet and oxygen mask and close down the two good engines before leaving my seat. As soon as I left the controls, however, the aircraft began to spin, making it a real struggle for me to get down and through the forward hatch.'

Somehow Geoff managed to exit before it was too late, but by now the Lancaster had lost further height and was dangerously close to the ground: 'I pulled the rip-cord straight away, but as the parachute opened, the harness, which I had not tightened enough, slipped off my shoulders and I found myself hanging upside down with everything falling out of my pockets and whizzing past my ears.'

For a few brief moments Geoff was in perilous danger. But a combination of strength and adrenaline saved the day as he managed to curl himself upwards into a U-shape and grab the harness just as the earth rushed up to meet him: 'I landed heavily on my backside but got away with it. In a parachute descent the parachute tends to swing, and I must have been on the upward curve at the point that I hit the

aircraft and landed in a water-filled ditch, lucky not to drown. For the time being, however, Geoff and Jack, the mid-upper gunner, and John, the bomb aimer, were still on the loose and considering their options.

The RAF crew brief included advice that the church was the best source of help in case of need and so, having seen a spire not far away, silhouetted by the flames of the crashed Lancaster, Geoff hid his parachute and headed that way. The remainder of his night was spent sitting on someone else's 'resting place' in the graveyard.

Left 'Missing.'
Geoffrey Packham

ground. It also helped that my touchdown point was a wheat field in full season, and that it was raining, so the ground was soft and muddy. Someone was obviously looking after me that night.'

Geoff had come down about a quarter of a mile from the village of Vlijmen and he took stock. Nearby, other members of his crew were doing the same but events were moving quickly. The aircraft had come down on a farmhouse, and with its bombs still on board the resultant explosion had been catastrophic, killing seven.

A party of German soldiers sent out to search for downed airmen was quick to round up the flight engineer, the wireless operator and one of the gunners. The navigator was also picked up and had been especially lucky. He had lost consciousness on leaving the

As dawn broke, Geoff sensed movement in the churchyard and saw what he took to be the vicar's wife. Soon after, he was explaining his situation to the vicar himself who fortunately spoke English. He also had contacts with an organised escape line. Sheltered in a series of safe houses, Geoff was given a suit and other civilian clothing as well as a forged identity card that claimed he was deaf and dumb. He was then moved 'down the line', walking, cycling and taking trains from Holland and into Belgium, and reunited with his mid-upper gunner along the way. On one overnight stay they found themselves in Breda, a leave centre for the German Army, but still remained undetected: 'We were escorted by couriers, each courier being close enough but far enough distant when we were travelling so that we did not appear together. We finally came to our last safe house, an apartment in Antwerp. We never knew the identity of the lady who looked after us but we ate well, even though food was very scarce, and were questioned again to confirm our own identities. We talked freely. We were told what would happen next. We were to be taken by ambulance into the country to rendezvous with the advancing allied army.'

With the food and the relative comfort, Geoff felt that it was all too good to be true. And so it proved. On the day they were due to leave, a large man came to call for them and escorted them downstairs and into a waiting car: 'He immediately pulled a gun on us and said "for you the war is over". Then he took us directly to the Germans.'

Neither Geoff nor Jack had any opportunity to escape, nor did they know at what point they had been betrayed. They had been ensnared in what was known as the 'KLM Line', a bogus escape line set up by German intelligence. Downed airmen who felt safe and among friends were inclined to talk, and unwittingly gave away military information that was otherwise very difficult to come by. The agent in charge of the operation was a Belgian, Rene van Muylem, who went under various aliases including Donald, Alfons and Mariant, and who worked in partnership with a young woman known only as 'Pauline'. More than 170 aircrew – both RAF and USAAF – went through van Muylem's hands and were betrayed, as were a large number of resistance workers. But whereas for the airmen it was interrogation and ultimately a prisoner of war camp, for the resistance it was invariably much worse.

As with the others who had been captured, Geoff and Jack were taken to Gestapo headquarters and thence onwards to Begijnenstraat prison for further cross-examination. At no stage were they harmed, but there was an implied threat throughout their questioning. It was at least a month before they were finally taken to Dulag Luft, after which they were separated. As an officer, Geoff was transferred to Stalag Luft I in Barth on the Baltic (he arrived on 3 August 1944) where he saw out the war. On the journey to Luft I a night-time stop was made in Frankfurt when an RAF raid on the city was about to take place. The small group of prisoners of war with whom Geoff was travelling was taken into a vast air-raid shelter for protection. They emerged later to a scene of utter devastation. 'That was the second time I'd been bombed – the first time had been by the Luftwaffe in Sheffield in 1940 when I helped my father, then an ART warden, put out the incendiary fires.'

Right The Boeing B17 Flying Fortress that brought Geoff home. *Geoffrey Packham*

Antwerp the 28 July 1945.

Dear Mister Packham,

I wonder if you still remember me from Antwerp, June 1944. You and M⁰ J. Jackson where hidden in my home a few days. Many things have happened since and I heard that you and your comrade Jackson have been made prisoner of war. I hope that you both are safely home now and that you are quite well. We also have had hard luck. Someone of our organisation betrayed us and we were arrested by the Gestapo and of course condemned to death. All this happened a few days before the liberation and that saved us because they had no time to execute us. I really owe my life to the Tommies who liberated Antwerp. Unfortunately the "Boches" took all we had.

Do you remember Nic the Russian

the attack on Sterkrade. Two other aircraft had also been lost, one of them flown by the 'B' Flight commander, Squadron Leader Gavin Smith, DFC. The second casualty was Flying Officer Donald Neilson's plane. Neilson, RCAF, and all of his crew were killed.

During Geoff's attempted evasion, his parents were fraught with worry. Often after an airman was shot down there would be some news through the International Red Cross, especially if he had been captured. But because Geoff was on the run for so long, there was nothing. The first time they knew that he was safe was much later, when his name was mentioned in a German radio broadcast by William Joyce, better known as 'Lord Haw-Haw'.

In 1945 Geoff came home to his happy, close-knit family and his job in Sheffield, his brother Peter arriving back from the Japanese war a little later. Geoff also returned to motorcycling,

Left 'We were arrested by the Gestapo and condemned to death.'
Geoffrey Packham

Stalag Luft I was liberated by the Russians on 1 May 1945, and Geoff was eventually flown home in an American B17 Flying Fortress, the former prisoners first having been required to help de-mine the Luftwaffe airfield.

While he was in the camp, Geoff was joined by two other officers from North Killingholme, Squadron Leader Kevin MacAleavey, DFC, and Flying Officer Beeson. MacAleavey was a navigator who had risen from sergeant to squadron leader in two years and commanded 'A' Flight. He had been flying in Beeson's crew when they were shot down on an attack on a V1 flying-bomb site during the evening of 28 August. The aircraft received a direct hit from flak and was seen to go down without any parachutes being observed. The ORB suggested at the time that 'it would appear that there are no survivors'. As it was, four of the crew did survive to become prisoners of war.

Through MacAleavey, Geoff learned that his crew had not been the only squadron casualties on

he also was arrested and very illtreated. He sends you his best regards. My son René also remembers you and sends you his kindest regards. If ever you come to Antwerp I shall be very happy to see you. I join a photo with this letter to remind you who I am. Please give my best regards to John Jackson. I hope to have news from you very soon and meanwhile I remain

Yours truly
M. Faitelson

M. Faitelson - Germain
53, rue Verdussen 53
Anvers - Belgique

P.S. Please excuse my bad English and bad spelling,

Right 'Mary' –
saint or sinner?
A young woman
caught up in the
complex world
of loyalty and
betrayal.
Geoffrey Packham

taking part, at weekends and in holidays, in a series of solo trials and sidecar events, teaming with his brother in a sidecar combination. Between them they competed all over the country, beating all but the very best – the very best being Eric Oliver, a four-time sidecar FIM world champion and one-time winner of the Isle of Man sidecar TT.

It was not until six years after the end of the war that Geoff managed to secure a job in commercial aviation as a pilot with the Belgian airline Sabena, with whom he enjoyed a long and successful career. He was one of only twelve to be selected out of hundreds of qualified pilots who applied. He later worked for the Civil Aviation Authority (CAA) as a senior flight operations inspector, still flying a variety of jet, turboprop and piston-engined aircraft, before finishing the role as part of the team that saw Concorde into commercial service.

To this day Geoff does not know for certain whether the lady who looked after him in the apartment in Antwerp was the same 'Pauline' who was jailed for twelve years for her part in betraying Allied airmen. He does, however, have a letter and a photograph sent to him shortly after the war by a lady named 'Mary' who wished to be remembered to him for her part in keeping Geoff and Jack safe in her apartment. She says that she was herself betrayed and condemned to death by the Gestapo, but only escaped execution thanks to the swift advance of the Allied armies.

Whatever the truth in the complex and often contradictory world of loyalty and betrayal in occupied Europe, Geoff viewed the episode as a great adventure. Many honest Dutch and Belgian helpers found themselves inadvertently caught up in van Muylem's web of intrigue and deceit, and he has the greatest admiration and gratitude for their bravery in assisting him and others.

At one point while on the run, Geoff wrote a letter to his parents that arrived in England only after the war had ended, in which he referred to his evasion as being 'an exciting escapade almost as fantastic as the stories and the films that are written about these things'. The letter concluded: 'All my hopes are centred on getting home.'

Happily, Geoff had only temporarily 'failed to return'. ●

Left The need for speed never left the Packham boys!
Geoffrey Packham

Left Geoff enjoyed a long and distinguished career after the war with the Belgian carrier, Sabena.
Geoffrey Packham

CHAPTER EIGHT

BROKEN LIVES

BY SEAN FEAST

NO. 460 SQUADRON RAAF HELD MANY RECORDS: IT WAS BELIEVED, FOR EXAMPLE, TO HAVE DROPPED THE HIGHEST TONNAGE OF BOMBS IN ALL OF BOMBER COMMAND. OUT OF THE AUSTRALIAN SQUADRONS IT CARRIED OUT THE MOST BOMBING RAIDS, FLEW THE MOST SORTIES, AND TOOK THE MOST LOSSES. AMONG THOSE WHO FAILED TO RETURN WAS THE CREW OF JACK ISRAEL, INCLUDING HIS WIRELESS OPERATOR, FRED BECKWITH.

D-DAY + 22. Operation Epsom is in full swing, an offensive to outflank and seize the vital city of Caen. Caen was an early objective of the invasion battle and now threatens to hold up the Allied advance. Meanwhile, around 300 kilometres to the east, the railway yards at Vaires on the outskirts of Paris are about to come in for the attention of a small force of Lancasters. The Pathfinders of 8 Group are unusually a few minutes late, and the first of the markers are not seen to go down until nearly three minutes after H-hour – the time of the attack.

Nineteen bombers from No. 460 Squadron Royal Australian Air Force (RAAF) are in a supporting role, all carrying 500lb bombs to cause maximum damage. The aircraft are stepped up between 11,000 and 14,000 feet and the first of their number begins bombing at 0302 hours, waits for the all-important photograph to check for accuracy and effect, and then heads for home. Enemy opposition over the target is negligible and the flak virtually non-existent, but the crews are still on the alert.

With throttles wide open it's a two-hour flight to RAF Binbrook in Lincolnshire, debriefing and then bed. Lancaster NE163 is one of the first to land at 0450 hours, Squadron Leader James Clark, DFC, at the controls. Clark will later go on to command the squadron and be killed in action in December 1944 over Essen. By 0522 hours, eighteen of the nineteen Lancasters have landed. One is not yet accounted for. It might still be possible that it has touched down elsewhere, and word has not yet come through. For the moment, Lancaster ME793 is 'missing'; soon after it is confirmed as outstanding, no news having been received since taking off. Telegrams are organised and dispatched to the next of kin, informing them that their loved ones have failed to return. One arrives at the home in Australia of the pilot, Jack Israel.

Closer to home, similar news is being reported to the wife of Israel's wireless operator, Fred Beckwith.

Frederick William Walter Beckwith was born on 12 September 1921 in Waterloo, south-east London. His family had been comparatively wealthy and his father had even spent time at Eton until the money ran out and their lives changed forever. Fred's childhood was spent primarily in Kennington, near to the Oval cricket ground. Indeed, he lived in Wisden House, named after the world-famous cricketing almanack. He was educated at the local Catholic school (St Anne's in Vauxhall), and despite, or perhaps because of, living in a city, Fred loved the outdoor life and would often plan camping excursions with his friends. Encouraged by his mother to box, he proved a successful junior boxer and was also a talented musician, entering and winning a local talent competition at the Grenada Cinema on the Wandsworth Road for his skills on the piano and piano accordion.

A good-looking young man, he found he was popular with the girls and one girl in particular, Edith, a near neighbour. Romance blossomed, and despite their youth the two were married on Boxing Day 1939. Their matrimony, however, coincided with dramatic events on the world stage and Fred – like thousands of others like him – felt compelled to answer his country's call and volunteered for aircrew training.

He enlisted on 1 December 1941, by which time his son Terry had been born, making the separation –

Left Fred Beckwith in full flying gear. *Beckwith family*

when it came – that much harder to take. But it was another six months before Fred was requested to attend No. 3 Recruitment Centre in Padgate (near Warrington) in June 1942 to receive his basic training. Within a few days he had moved to No. 10 Recruitment Centre to spend three months appreciating the fundamentals of signals including Morse, Aldis and flag, as well as the limitations of wireless communications. From Blackpool he was posted to No. 2 Signals & Wireless School at Yatesbury for operator training and ever more Morse, until March 1943. According to his record of service, Fred returned to Yatesbury in May 1943 before proceeding to No. 3 Advanced Flying Unit (AFU) to become familiarised with the first stages of instruction for actual operations.

It was at 28 Operational Training Unit (OTU), however, at RAF Wymeswold in Leicestershire that he finally became part of a real crew, and met the other 'trades' – the navigator, air bomber, air gunner and of course the pilot on which his life could depend.

His skipper was a twenty-year-old Australian from Kogarah, a suburb of southern Sydney in New South Wales. He had made it through to four engines despite a mishap early in his training when he crashed a Tiger Moth. The air bomber was another Australian, Gregory Hunkin, from Numurkah, Victoria. He was also twenty. The navigator, flight engineer and one of the two air gunners were English: Leo Pester was from Plymouth; Leslie George from Sunbury-on-Thames; and Albert Rouse was from Essex. The second air gunner, and the only other officer in the crew, was Canadian. He was twenty-year-old Tony Krynski from Manitoba.

The crew spent more than four months at OTU, flying clapped-out Wellingtons in operational conditions, or at least as close as wartime instruction allowed. Night-time cross-country flights and daytime lectures were the order of the day, as crews endeavoured to learn every facet of life on an operational squadron. Towards the end of their training, these

Left Fred loved the outdoor life and would often plan camping excursions with his friends.
Beckwith family

cross-country trips involved flying close to or even over the French coast, acting as 'decoys' for main-force raids to deceive the enemy radar controllers, or to drop leaflets on the occupied peoples.

Eventually posted to 11 Base – the 'Base' system comprising one main and two satellite airfields under the command of an air commodore, having been introduced to improve levels of communication and control – the airmen bided their time until a request came through for a replacement crew. That request eventually arrived in the second week of May from the commanding officer of No. 460 Squadron.

No. 460 Squadron RAAF was what was known as an Article XV squadron, allowing for the formation of distinct Dominion squadrons in the RAF's Order of Battle. Australian, Canadian and New Zealand airmen trained under the Empire Training Scheme would therefore be able to serve in Australian, Canadian and New Zealand squadrons, but the British retained control of all command appointments and promotions.

Formed on 15 November 1941 at RAF Molesworth, for expediency aircrew and indeed ground personnel were originally found from RAF sources, except where RAAF personnel were immediately available. Originally flying twin-engined Wellingtons, the squadron began converting to the four-engined Halifax in the autumn of 1942, but by the time Fred and the others arrived it was operating Lancasters from RAF Binbrook as part of 1 Group. The officer commanding No. 460 Squadron was Wing Commander John Douglas, who had taken over command from Wing Commander Horton Marsh in the same week that Fred and his colleagues joined the squadron. (Wing Commander Douglas, DFC, AFC, was an experienced bomber captain who later went on to command No. 467 Squadron RAAF before being killed on operations on 8 February 1945; Wing Commander Marsh rose to the rank of air commodore and was awarded the DFC as OC of No. 38 Squadron RAAF during the Malayan Emergency.)

The squadron had sustained heavy casualties in the weeks preceding the crew's arrival, hence the need for replacements. Indeed, over Mailly-le-Camp on 3/4 May, it had lost no fewer than six aircraft and thirty-nine men in a single attack.

Despite the need to rapidly rebuild the squadron's strength, the Israel team was not immediately detailed for operations. It was customary for any new crew, when conditions allowed, to be afforded a brief period to 'bed in' with additional training and local cross-country flights. It was usual, also, for the pilot to fly a one-off 'second dickey' flight with another more experienced crew before taking his own men on operations, but this was not always possible. On 27 May the crew was excited to see their names posted on the Battle Order for that evening's operation, an attack on the gun emplacement at Merville.

halfway through their tour, failed to return, despite the defences being described as 'non-existent'.

Another field battery was singled out for attack the following night and again the raid was a success. Jack Israel's aircrew in Lancaster LM530 (which also survived the war) again returned home having bombed the centre of the markers.

With the invasion just a week away, the bombing of gun emplacements, radar installations and transport hubs intensified, both in the 'real' invasion area and the Pas de Calais, to keep up the pretence that the shortest hop across the Channel was still the pre-

Right
Three classes at the wireless ops' training school at RAF Yatesbury, March 1943. Fred is top row, second from left.
Beckwith family

Merville was one of the more high-profile German gun positions and the scene on D-Day of a heroic attack by British paratroopers that has gone down in history. On the night of 27/28 May, the squadron dispatched twenty of their number to saturate the defences with a mixture of 1,000lb and 500lb bombs on an operation that was considered by the author of the squadron Operations Record Book (ORB) as being 'a satisfactory raid'. For the Israel crew in Lancaster ND392 (which survived the war), the flight went without a hitch. Greg Hunkin, the air bomber, was easily able to pick out one of the red spot fires and reported 'one direct hit'. They returned safely to land at Binbrook at 0404 hours. Not everyone was so lucky: Pilot Officer Ronald Kirkland and his crew, who were

ferred option for breaking Rommel's infamous Atlantic Wall. After an attack on Berneval-le-Grand on 2/3 June, in which the Israel crew took part, there were further assaults on both the eve of D-Day and D-Day itself, with raids on Saint-Martin-de-Varreville and Vire.

Fred and his colleagues came through all three sorties unscathed, but others in the squadron had rather more excitement. A number of crews came into conflict with night fighters over Berneval. The gunners within ND174 (Flight Sergeants Halsall and O'Leary within the crew of Pilot Officer S. J. Davey) saw discretion as the better part of valour and opened fire on a Focke Wulf Fw190 before the surprised German pilot had time to respond. It might possibly have been the same fighter that fifteen minutes earlier had attacked Lancaster ME793 (flown by Warrant Officer White) and similarly been repelled without inflicting any damage. Flight Sergeant Denniston and Sergeant Moody in NE163 (with Flight Sergeant Lutton at the controls) opened fire on yet another Fw190 on the night of 6 June and claimed the aircraft as damaged. While these airmen escaped, and indeed went on to complete their tours, Pilot Officer Frederick Knight, RAAF, and his crew were not so lucky, being shot down and killed over Vire.

With the first five operations now under their belts,

the Israel crew's confidence was beginning to build. The casualty rate had mercifully slowed, and with experience came an increased chance of survival. Two more raids on the Forêt de Cerisy and the marshalling yards at Évreux – the latter at a height of only 2,000 feet – were followed by the crew's first visit to Germany. The Nordstern synthetic oil plant near Gelsenkirchen was the chosen target for more than 300 bombers, 14 of which came from No. 460 Squadron.

Greg Hunkin would have been surprised and gratified by his bombload: as well as the usual mix of 500-pounders, each aircraft was also to carry one of the 4,000lb 'Cookies' – a high-capacity Amatol-based 'blockbuster' – in the bomb bay. All of the squadron aircraft got away safely and in fair weather, the Israel crew in Lancaster JB743 (one of the longest-serving aircraft on the squadron) taking off at 2308 hours for the comparatively short but invariably dangerous trip to the Ruhr. Although the contemporary ORB and subsequent post-raid reports suggest some confusion

in both the marking and the bombing caused by a rogue target indicator (TI), the attack overall was a notable success, and oil production halted almost entirely for several weeks. Hunkin dropped his 'Cookie' and smaller bombs on a green TI at 0108, and seemed happy with the result. Their aircraft landed safely back at 0253 hours. But one of their number was missing: Pilot Officer Austin Roche, RAAF, and his crew were all killed only a handful of trips short of completing their first tour.

While the squadron took part in an attack on Le Havre on 14/15 June, the Israel crew was rested, and no doubt took full advantage of their temporary respite. The men had pooled together to buy a car, and it proved a vital link with the outside world. Time off the base was precious, and crews would usually stick together to drink at the local bars and hotels in nearby Grimsby, or pair off to visit friends and family. The Australians, Canadians and other Commonwealth airmen were especially grateful for the chance of some home comforts, being so far away from their loved ones themselves. In return they were only too pleased to share their food parcels, that added more variety to the local 'fare'.

For Fred and his young wife Edith, the separation forced upon them by war was bewildering. They now had two children (Terry had been joined by his sister Jean in 1942) and the stresses of bringing up a young family alone was difficult enough in peacetime, but even more of a challenge when any moment Edith might hear the knock on the door and be handed the message she would refuse to believe. For Fred, too, the enormity of it all must have been hard to grasp. Many wrote at the time, and have spoken about since, the strange contrast of one minute being over Germany, in fear for your life, and the next, tucked up in a warm bed or down the pub drinking with your best and most important friends.

Boulogne was attacked on the night of 15/16 June, with twenty-two squadron aircraft taking part. It was a short trip of only two and a half hours and all returned safely, having successfully found and bombed the target. On 16/17 June the focus changed to one of the flying-bomb construction sites in Domleger.

Left Fred with his No. 460 Squadron crew. Identifiable are: Sergeant Leslie White (foreground) and Sergeant Leo Pester (left foreground); Pilot Officer Jack Israel (in cockpit front) with Fred (in cockpit behind); Greg Hunkin (on nose, slightly obscured). The two airmen to the left are most likely the sergeant air gunners Tony Krynski and Albert Rouse. *Beckwith family*

Cloud obscured the target, and the crews did their best to bomb the red TIs dropped by the Pathfinder Mosquitoes using the blind bombing device, Oboe. Opposition was slight, and once again all of the squadron aircraft returned home safely. Two 500lb bombs in the Lancaster of Pilot Officer Neville Twyford (later Flying Officer, DFC) 'hung up', but other than that there was little to report.

After a welcome pause, the squadron was again briefed for operations on the night of 22/23 June and contributed twenty-one of its aircraft to an attack on the railway marshalling yards at Rheims. It proved to be a costly affair. The Israel team once more returned without incident but two crews were missing, those of thirty-year-old Flying Officer Francis Lamble, RAAF, and Flight Sergeant Laurence Pearson, RAAF, who was twenty-seven. While the ORB describes the trip as 'quiet and uneventful', night fighters most probably accounted for both of the squadron aircraft shot down that night, Lamble being the victim of Oberleutnant Walter Riedlberger of I/NJG4 for his ninth victory and Pearson falling foul of Feldwebel Doll of II/NJG3 for his first 'viermot' (four-motor) kill.

At least two other crews also reported fighter activity: Pilot Officer H. F. Korsman, flying in Lancaster LL905, found his aircraft under attack around fifteen minutes short of the target and threw the heavy bomber into a 'corkscrew' – the standard evasive manoeuvre at the time. The unidentified enemy aircraft opened fire with two bursts, but was almost immediately hit by return fire from the rear gunner. The night fighter caught fire and was shortly after seen to hit the ground and explode. (Korsman completed thirty-one operations with No. 460 Squadron.) Fifteen minutes later, the Lancaster of Pilot Officer Lewis found itself the intended victim of a single-engined Messerschmitt Bf109 and twin-engined Junkers Ju88 that appeared to be working in tandem, the Bf109 attacking from behind and the Ju88 head-on. Unusually, the rear gunner, mid-upper gunner and the air bomber manning the front turret were all involved in the battle that ensued, the air bomber claiming hits on the Junkers. Having successfully fought off the first assault the Lancaster was again singled out by a pair of Fw190s, with one attacking and the second appearing to act as decoy. Through skilful manoeuvring the pilot was able to lose both aircraft and the Lancaster disappeared into the night.

Two more operations followed for the Israel crew: one was a daylight raid to the flying-bomb launch site at Les Hayons; the second was a similar daylight in the early morning to Ligescourt. The former was particularly noteworthy, for one of the nineteen Lancasters involved was flown by the station commander of RAF Binbrook, Group Captain Hughie Edwards, VC, DSO, DFC. The group captain chose to fly with the crew of Pilot Officer G. T. Stone in what was rumoured to be his 109th operation. Edwards had won the Victoria Cross in 1941 as OC No. 105 Squadron for a daring low-level attack on the port of Bremen and had assumed command of Binbrook in February 1943. Despite his senior rank, Edwards was a man who still believed in leading from the front. The raid was completed without incident.

On the latter sortie, the aircraft returned to find that the weather had closed in. Rain was lashing across the airfield and the cloud base was down to about 200 feet. Scores of station personnel emerged at the sound of Merlins and to watch events unfold. Miraculously, although not without a few close shaves, all of the aircraft managed to make it down in one piece. A2 'Aussie' (Lancaster ND392), flown by Warrant Officer George Lindenberg, returned with a hole in the mainplane big enough for a man to crawl through. (Lindenberg, who had worked in a sawmill before the war, was shot at over Caen a few weeks later and survived the crash-landing that resulted. By the end of his tour of thirty operations he had been commissioned and awarded the DFC.)

On 27 June, a request was received from Group headquarters for the squadron to contribute nineteen aircraft for an attack that night on the railway yards at Vaires to the east of Paris. Pilot Officer Jack Israel and his regular crew were on the Battle Order for what would be their fourteenth operation – almost halfway through an operational tour of thirty. If the pace of operations had continued at that rate, they might reasonably have expected to have finished their tour before the summer was out.

Pilot Officer Ronald Tardent (later DFC) was the first to get away at 0036 hours, closely followed by one of the flight commanders, Squadron Leader James Clark. Almost twenty minutes later the last of the squadron aircraft had left the ground and made its way to the assembly area. H-hour was 0300, and the first of the Pathfinder target indicators was slightly early. While most of the crews were happy that they had achieved a good concentration of bombs in the target area, their satisfaction was tempered by the news that one of their number was missing: ME793 had failed to return.

What happened to the Lancaster and the crew of ME793 is not known with any certainty. While none of the No. 460 Squadron crews operating that night appear to have submitted combat reports, suggesting a lack of night-fighter activity, this is not to say that the night fighters were not about. Dr Theo Boiten in his *Nachtjagd War Diaries* suggests that one of either two pilots may have accounted for Fred's Lancaster: Helmut Lent of Stab NJG3 for his 103rd 'kill' or Jakob Schaus of IV/NJG4 for his 18th. (Lent was at the time the top-scoring Luftwaffe night-fighter pilot and would finish his war with a total of 110 kills before losing his own life in a crash-landing in October 1944. Schaus, too, did not survive to see peace, being shot down by an RAF intruder in February the following year.)

But there is also another possibility. In the con-temporary diary of Cliff Halsall, a No. 460 Squadron air gunner, he states that 'it was thought that [the] Lancaster had blown up near The Wash on the way out'. This was certainly a popular rumour at the time, and one repeated after the war by one of the ground crew personnel to the family. He suggested that ME793 had collided with a smaller aircraft. Had that been the case, the result on an aircraft packed with fuel and explosives would have been catastrophic.

In crowded skies, with hundreds of aircraft making their way to the same point at the same time, accidents did most certainly happen. Collisions were uncommon, but not unheard of. The only other aircraft lost on the Vaires operation came down over enemy territory, however, which appears to rule out a collision with an aircraft on the same raid. That is not to say that their aircraft was not hit by another heading for a different target, but again it is unlikely. As for the rumour of a smaller aircraft, this can only be conjecture. Whatever the cause, Fred Beckwith and the crew of Jack Israel had taken their final flight, and died together. They are remembered on the Runnymede Memorial. ●

Left Fred's children, Terry and Jean, at their mother's grave, commemorating their late father.
Beckwith family

CHAPTER NINE

BOMBING, BETRAYAL AND BUCHENWALD

BY PETER COOK

ON 28/29 JUNE 1944 HALIFAX BOMBERS OF NO. 102 SQUADRON WERE SENT TO THE RAIL MARSHALLING YARDS AT BLAINVILLE-SUR-L'EAU. EARLIER THAT DAY AT THE ALLIED AIR COMMANDERS' CONFERENCE THERE HAD BEEN CONSIDERABLE OPTIMISM CONCERNING THE BOMBING ATTACKS ON GERMAN COMMUNICATIONS. ENEMY PRISONERS, UNDER INTERROGATION, HAD REPORTED ON THE SERIOUS DISRUPTION TO REINFORCEMENTS. THE FOLLOWING DAY ALLIED EXPEDITIONARY AIR FORCE COMMANDER AIR MARSHAL SIR TRAFFORD LEIGH MALLORY RECORDED IN HIS DIARY: 'LAST NIGHT, THANK HEAVEN, BOMBER COMMAND ATTACKED METZ AND BLAINVILLE AND THIS RELIEVED MY MIND A LOT. ... THEY ARE VERY IMPORTANT TRAIN CENTRES AT THE MOMENT.' BUT THE PRICE HAD BEEN HIGH, WITH TWENTY AIRCRAFT LOST. FIVE NO. 102 SQUADRON AIRCRAFT FAILED TO RETURN. REG JOYCE HAD BEEN IN THE REAR TURRET OF HALIFAX LW143.

REGINALD WILLIAM JOYCE was born on 12 February 1925 in the now east London district of Stratford. He lost his father at the tender age of eight and through other family circumstances went to live with a paternal aunt and her family in nearby Walthamstow. Among Reg's cousins in the household was Frederick John Nicoll, who in 1944 would earn a Distinguished Flying Cross piloting rocket-firing Hurricanes, primarily over the Adriatic and Balkans. Prior to joining up Reg was employed as a junior clerk and had already shown early signs of air-mindedness by having been a cadet in the fledgling Air Training Corps, an organisation newly established in 1941 from the former Air Defence Cadet Corps. Reg had no doubt as to which of the three services he wanted to serve in and at the age of seventeen, rather than wait for his call-up papers, he volunteered for the Royal Air Force.

On 21 December 1942 Reg enlisted in the RAF having been passed medically fit the previous June.

The following day he was posted to the Reserve and subsequently attended an Aircrew Selection Board (ACSB) on 27 December, but was not at this time recommended for aircrew duties. He was eventually recalled from the Reserve on 16 February 1943, just days after his eighteenth birthday. On 25 July 1943, following a period of training and a short posting with No. 183 Squadron, Reg remustered as an air gunner under training and attended the Aircrew Reception Centre (ACRC) at Abbey Lodge, in London's Regent's Park. On 7 August he joined No. 14 Initial Training Wing (ITW) at Bridlington and thereafter progressed to No. 1 Elementary Air Gunners School (EAGS) at Bridgnorth, joining on 11 September. Next stop was No. 7 Air Gunners School (AGS) at RAF Stormy Down, where from 2 October he attended 121 Air Gunnery Course, eventually earning his air gunner's brevet on 19 November with a pass mark of 71.6%.

On 23 November Reg was posted to No. 20 Operational Training Unit (OTU) at RAF Lossiemouth, where he was crewed up with five of the individuals (the flight engineer joining after OTU) who would effectively share his life from that moment on, or at least up until a fateful June night in 1944. It was a mix of nationalities that eventually made up the crew, consisting of three Englishmen, two Australians and two Canadians. With Reg occupying the inhospitable position of rear gunner, the final complement would comprise: pilot Nigel Douglas Campbell, RAAF, a twenty-year-old Australian and former clerk from Toowoomba in the state of Queensland; navigator Arthur Douglas Eagle, RAF, aged twenty-seven and a former quantity surveyor's assistant from Birmingham; bomb aimer Jack Wilson, RCAF, a Canadian in his early twenties from Prince Albert, Saskatchewan; wireless operator Noel Albert Pardon, RAAF, a twenty-year-old Australian and former student from Camberwell in the state of Victoria; mid-upper air gunner Ronald Lambert Leverington, RAF, who was twenty-three and a former rent and wages clerk from Deal in Kent; and flight engineer Donald Eugene Leslie, a Canadian aged twenty-two and a former student from Vancouver, British Columbia, who had joined the RAF straight after high school, initially as a Halton Apprentice.

From the OTU the crew were attached to 4 Group's Battle School at RAF Driffield, where they learned

Left Nigel Campbell.
Jeff Boyling via the Campbell family

rudimentary military skills and escape and evasion techniques, disciplines that four of them would all too soon be putting into practice for real. The final leg of their training commenced on 31 March 1944, when the crew were attached to No. 1652 Heavy Conversion Unit (HCU) at RAF Marston Moor, for conversion on to the stalwart Handley Page Halifax, the mainstay of 4 Group at that time.

Inevitably, the end of their training heralded in the long-anticipated posting to an operational front-line bomber squadron, and the commencement of an unpredictable tour in what was then one of the most dangerous occupations ever evolved in modern warfare. Aerial bombing had in a few short years claimed lives on an unprecedented scale, for both those who flew in the bombers and those unfortunates who would get to 'reap the whirlwind' at the reception end of the strategic offensive. Reg and his crewmates were elevated to the forefront of that flying war when on 30 May 1944 they were posted to No. 102 (Ceylon) Squadron, based at RAF Pocklington in North Yorkshire. Then equipped with Halifax

IIIs, the squadron formed part of 4 Group and was destined to end the war with the third highest casualty rate in Bomber Command.

For Bomber Command, 25 June 1944 was to be another all-out effort aimed at destroying the VI flying-bomb menace that had daily been causing fear and destruction in the south of England; it was also the day that Reg and his crewmates appeared on a Battle Order for the first time. This maiden mission was for some of the crew the culmination of almost two years of intensive training, though in Reg's case it equated to exactly eleven months since he had remustered as a trainee air gunner. No. 4 Group's contribution on this day would consist of 101 aircraft detailed for a daylight attack against the VI site located at Montorgueil, in the Pas-de-Calais area of northern France; 18 of the force would be Halifaxes of No. 102 Squadron. (From a historical perspective, the previous day had seen only the second ever daylight operation mounted by the squadron since 3 August 1942, when a mission to Hamburg had been aborted, ironically due to a lack of cloud.)

Right No. 4 Group Battle School. Centre row, left are the crew of LW143, from left to right: Nigel Campbell, Noel Pardon, Reg Joyce, Ron Leverington, Arthur Eagle and Jack Wilson.
Jeff Boyling via the Campbell family

Left Jack Wilson, Nigel Campbell and Noel Pardon. *Jeff Boyling via the Campbell family*

With Nigel Campbell at the controls, the wheels of the Halifax became 'unstuck' from Pocklington's runway at 0752 hours and Arthur Eagle systematically guided the pilot on towards the target at Montorgueil. The round trip would last less than four hours and they eventually touched back down at Pocklington at 1146 hours, their debut trip to the continent at an end. The details of their sortie were recorded in the squadron ORB as: 'Clear over target. Red T.I. seen on approach. Bombed on red T.I. and visual. 17000 feet heading 130°T 175 IAS. Bursts seen in target area. 11 x 500 GP 2 x 500 GP LD.' The operational order sent out by Headquarters 4 Group prior to the raid had specified the required bombload to be 'Buffer' with two of the 500lb general-purpose bombs to be fused long delay six to thirty-six hours. A sober-

ing prospect for anybody sent in to clear up in the raid's aftermath.

Headquarters 4 Group proclaimed the attack a success, although two aircraft were missing, one from No. 102 Squadron and the other from No. 77 Squadron. There are a number of recorded accounts summarising the unfortunate fate of the aircraft lost from this mission, including several No. 102 Squadron crews reporting seeing a Halifax either exploding or disintegrating over the target area. One seemingly unquestionable source (from a rear gunner of an involved No. 10 Squadron Halifax) claims that he saw the bombs dropped from his aircraft tragically hitting another plane. This then broke up and its wing struck the No. 102 Squadron Halifax, which then exploded.

It may not have been a taxing assignment for many seasoned crews, but as far as Reg and his mates were concerned they had broken their duck and got home safely. In line with Air Ministry policy during this period, for 'soft or easy targets' in France, the outing would only count as one-third of an operational sortie towards the bewildering thirty they were required to complete. However, thirty was a distant goal and statistically, as a rookie crew, they would be lucky to survive as many as five missions. They were not four days away from confirming those odds.

Newly blooded, the crew next appeared on a Battle Order for an attack against the V1 launching site at Mont Candon in northern France, scheduled for the

Left Picture taken by flight engineer Don Leslie, left to right: Noel Pardon, Ronald Leverington, Arthur ('Doug') Eagle, Jack Wilson, Nigel Campbell and Reginald Joyce. *Jeff Boyling via the Campbell Family.*

On this night twenty aircraft from the squadron would be detailed to attack the railway marshalling yards at Blainville-sur-l'Eau, five of which would fail to return. Of the aircrew that set off in those five doomed Halifaxes, nineteen were destined to die and sixteen survive. Of those survivors half would successfully evade capture and return to the UK, while the remaining eight would eventually become prisoners of war. Six of those, including Reg and three crewmates, would for a period number among 168 Allied airmen from Britain, the Commonwealth and the USA, who were illegally incarcerated in the infamous Buchenwald concentration camp. That the majority would live to tell the tale of their ordeal is a story of luck, heroism and the surprise intervention by one of the most unlikely of benefactors in Nazi authority.

It was 2157 hours on 28 June 1944 when Nigel Campbell once again, and for the last time, eased his laden Halifax into the air from Pocklington. The following morning there would be no post-op interrogation for the crew back at base. Alongside their aircraft and four others from the squadron the ORB would simply be annotated: 'Aircraft missing no news after take-off.'

night of 27/28 June 1944. At debriefing the crew claimed what they believed to have been another successful sortie, recorded in the ORB as: 'Clear over target. Red T.I. on run up. 16300 feet heading 240°T 185 IAS. All bombs on target. Bombed red T.I. PFF very good. 14 x 500 GP 2 x 500 GP LD.' However, from an overall perspective 4 Group deemed the raid only partially successful. Notwithstanding this, the crew had once more returned unscathed, though again they would only be credited with one-third of an op. Their operational tally now totalling two-thirds of a single sortie was academic, though, as within twenty hours of landing from this raid they would once again take to the air on what would prove to be their final flight of the war. In less than twenty-four hours three of the seven would be dead.

The night of 28/29 June 1944 was to prove costly to Bomber Command as a whole, but as far as No. 102 Squadron was concerned it would be devastating in terms of aircraft lost and aircrew killed or missing.

As the Halifax flew ever closer on to the target, Reg recalled Noel Pardon reporting over the intercom that he had spotted another aircraft behind their bomber. Pilot Nigel Campbell responded that it was probably another Halifax, but still ordered the crew to keep their eyes peeled. Soon after the initial sighting Reg observed an approaching aircraft, which he believed to be a Messerschmitt Bf110. Both Reg and the German night fighter opened fire at the same time, but before Reg could register any mark on the enemy aircraft it had overflown his rear turret and scored hits in the left wing of the Halifax that in turn caused the wing fuel tank to ignite. Miraculously, Reg was blessed with sufficient time to reach back into the fuselage and grab his parachute, which he hurriedly attached to his chest harness. He was in the last throes of rotating his tail turret to make good his escape when, as he describes, 'the aircraft exploded', launching him into the night sky.

With his parachute successfully deployed Reg completed an uneventful descent to earth, although minus his flying boots and socks. He had been lucky to say the least and the only injury he sustained from the shooting-down was a burn to his chin, which if not life-threatening did prove significant enough to prevent whiskers ever growing again from the area of damaged tissue.

While events had been dramatically unfolding in the night sky above, a young French girl had stood with her mother on the roof of the local village store, both witnessing the dying moments of LW143 and the parachute descents of the escaping crew. The name of that girl was Janine Colzy and what Reg could never have contemplated at that moment in time was that fate would one day bring them into contact again. Against all reasonable odds, in just over five years from that eventful night, Reg and Janine would become man and wife.

Regarding the fate of the rest of the crew immediately after the aerial combat, it is believed that Noel Pardon and Jack Wilson were both dead in the aircraft, while Arthur Eagle, Ron Leverington and Don Leslie were successful in baling out. As for pilot Nigel Campbell, it is evident that he was still alive after the combat, as he gave the order for the surviving crew to abandon their stricken bomber. This was further confirmed shortly after the war, when Nigel's mother was sent letters and photos by his surviving crewmates, who had returned to France post-hostilities and visited the primary crash site of LW143. One of the letters explained that two of the crew were dead in the aircraft before the remaining four had parachuted, and that Nigel had kept control of the aircraft as they made their exit. Unfortunately, by the time Nigel himself managed to abandon the aircraft there was insufficient height for his parachute to save him and he landed in a tree, which had to be cut down to retrieve his body.

Nigel had performed his duty to the heroic last, ensuring the survival of his crew before ever considering his own safety. He will forever be numbered among that unquantifiable band of unsung heroes, whose families in most cases would never know the truth of their loved one's last deed, nor be presented with a richly deserved decoration that might in some way have served as a comforting memorial to their selfless courage and ultimate sacrifice.

Through extant official records and the personal testimonies of those who survived the downing of LW143, it is possible to elaborate further on some of the details surrounding their last mission and the aftermath of being shot down over enemy territory. Following the end of the war, all released and repatriated prisoners of war from Britain and the Commonwealth were subjected to a post-release interrogation by IS9 (No. 9 Intelligence School), the executive branch of MI9 (Section 9 of Military Intelligence). While the IS9 reports were compiled around sixteen months after the start of their ordeal, the survivors of LW143 were questioned at the earliest opportunity after repatriation, when their memories would have been freshest. As with any eyewitness accounts, though, an individual's recollections can vary either slightly or considerably from those of others who saw or experienced the same event, and there are understandably some minor inconsistencies apparent between some of the recorded events. Arthur, Ron and Don provided reports, and relevant extracts follow (none existing for Reg, however; his IS9 report literally comprises a copy of Don's

Right Document from the North Compound at Stalag Luft III recording the arrival of Reg Joyce and colleagues from Buchenwald.
Peter Cook

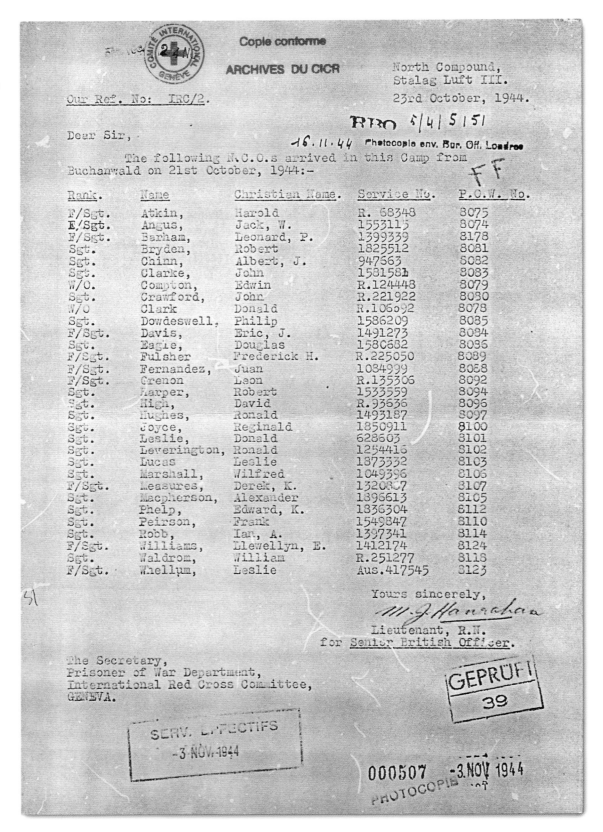

Copie conforme

ARCHIVES DU CICR

North Compound,
Stalag Luft III.
23rd October, 1944.

Our Ref. No: IRC/2.

RBO 5/4/5151

Dear Sir,

16.11.44 Photocopie env. Bor. Off. Londres

The following N.C.O.s arrived in this Camp from Buchanwald on 21st October, 1944:-

FF

Rank.	Name	Christian Name.	Service No.	P.O.W. No.
F/Sgt.	Atkin,	Harold	R. 68348	8075
F/Sgt.	Angus,	Jack, W.	1553115	8074
F/Sgt.	Barham,	Leonard, P.	1399339	8178
Sgt.	Bryden,	Robert	1825512	8081
Sgt.	Chinn,	Albert, J.	947663	8082
Sgt.	Clarke,	John	1581581	8083
W/O.	Compton,	Edwin	R.124448	8079
Sgt.	Crawford,	John	R.221922	8080
W/O	Clark	Donald	R.106592	8078
Sgt.	Dowdeswell,	Philip	1586209	8085
F/Sgt.	Davis,	Eric, J.	1491273	8084
Sgt.	Eagle,	Douglas	1580682	8086
F/Sgt.	Fulsher	Frederick H.	R.225050	8089
F/Sgt.	Fernandez,	Juan	1084999	8088
F/Sgt.	Grenon	Leon	R.135306	8092
Sgt.	Harper,	Robert	1533559	8094
Sgt.	High,	David	R.93636	8096
Sgt.	Hughes,	Ronald	1493187	8097
Sgt.	Joyce,	Reginald	1850911	8100
Sgt.	Leslie,	Donald	628603	8101
Sgt.	Leverington,	Ronald	1254416	8102
Sgt.	Lucas	Leslie	1873332	8103
Sgt.	Marshall,	Wilfred	1049396	8106
F/Sgt.	Measures,	Derek, K.	1320857	8107
Sgt.	Macpherson,	Alexander	1896613	8105
Sgt.	Phelp,	Edward, K.	1836304	8112
Sgt.	Peirson,	Frank	1549847	8110
Sgt.	Robb,	Ian, A.	1397341	8114
F/Sgt.	Williams,	Llewellyn, E.	1412174	8124
Sgt.	Waldrom,	William	R.251277	8118
F/Sgt.	Whellum,	Leslie	Aus.417545	8123

Yours sincerely,

M.J.Hanrahan

Lieutenant, R.N.
for Senior British Officer.

The Secretary,
Prisoner of War Department,
International Red Cross Committee,
GENEVA.

GEPRÜFT
39

SERV. EFFECTIFS
- 3 NOV. 1944

000507 - 3 NOV 1944
PHOTOCOPIE

testimony, their experiences having been deemed so similar).

Ron Leverington's account states:

We took off from Pocklington in a Halifax aircraft at 2230 hrs on 28 Jun 44 on a bombing mission to Blaineville [sic]. On the way to the target the aircraft was attacked by an Me110. The controls were damaged and the port inner engine caught fire. The order to abandon aircraft was given and I bailed out. Three members of the crew were killed and three successfully baled out.

I landed in a forest at Lyons-La-Foret, South of Rouen at 0030 hrs. I ricked my neck on landing and lost consciousness for about 15 minutes. When I came to I hid my parachute under some logs and my helmet in the hollow of a tree. I had dropped my escape kit on landing, so decided to wait until daylight. I slept until dawn and found my escape kit a few yards away. I found a farm and by hiding in some bushes watched it all day. In the evening a farmer (name unknown) came as he had seen me. He spoke to me in French and I made him understand I was R.A.F. He took me to a dugout behind a barn and gave me food and a pair of boots as I had lost mine when baling out. I stayed in the dugout for two days.

Arthur Eagle's report notes: ' The port wing took fire and the captain gave the order to bail out. The pilot, bomb-aimer and wireless operator were killed and the rest of us landed safely, although I was knocked unconscious in jumping. When I regained consciousness I hid my parachute and lay up the whole of the next day and night.'

Regarding the identity of the Luftwaffe pilot responsible for the fate of LW143, all evidence points towards Major Paul Semrau of Stab II/NJG2, who claimed four heavies shot down in the early hours of 29 June, all within the space of just under half an hour. Semrau would go on to achieve a personal tally of forty-six nocturnal victories before being killed in action on 8 February 1945. (While the crew of LW143 believe that it was a Messerschmitt Bf110 that had sealed their fate, the aircraft type operated by II/NJG2 at the time was actually the Junkers Ju88.)

For each of the four survivors, alone and in enemy-occupied territory, the story now turns to one of evasion. While their time spent at the 4 Group Battle School was designed to prepare them for this eventuality, it is still difficult to comprehend the emotions an evader in his late teens or early twenties might

have been experiencing after parachuting from a burning Halifax. They were in the dark, disorientated and not knowing who they could trust, plus three of their closest companions were dead.

Ron Leverington's account continues:

On 31 [sic] Jun the farmer gave me some more food and at 0100 hrs I left the farm, walking due West intending to reach the British lines. I was wearing a pullover over my R.A.F. uniform. My neck was still hurting me and I only managed to walk about five kms that night. After walking for about an hour I found I was quite close to a village (name unknown).

I thought it inadvisable to enter the village in daylight. I remained in a field on the outskirts until 1200 hrs, then decided to make a detour of the village. Passing a farm I met a man on a water wagon. He stopped and seemed quite friendly. He told me to climb up beside him on the wagon and I rode through the village with him. He directed me to a little hideout in a hedge and told me to stay there. He returned two hours later with two Frenchmen. One of the Frenchmen, a former French Army officer, took me to a little woodshed on the edge of the forest. He told me to stay there and suggested that a few hours later I should go with him to the other side of the forest where another member of the R.A.F. (F/O Hemens?) [sic] was also hiding. I stayed in the woodshed until evening, when he returned, bringing with him some food, an old mackintoch [sic], a beret, and a garden rake. I dressed in the clothes and with the rake over my shoulder followed him deep into the forest. He took me to a small barn and told me to wait until he returned. I went to sleep and at midnight I awoke to find my navigator had arrived. We both spent the night there. On 2 Jul the Frenchman took us through the forest. We started walking at 0800 hrs and walked for four hrs. He took us to a cave where he told us to stay until someone came for us. After two hours a French lady, who could speak perfect English, came, bringing us a hot meal. She said she was hiding the two other members of my crew and also the other member of the R.A.F. (F/O Hemens) [sic]. We remained in her house until 7 Aug.

Arthur Eagle's statement recalls:

On the 30 Jun I contacted a farmer in the village of Goupillere, who hid me and fed me for two or three days. The farmer's son then guided me to the village of Beaufical where I stayed one night with the local resistance leaders. I there met Sgt Leverington R. of our crew. On about 4 Jul we were guided to a hamlet called Mortemer on the fringe of the Foret de Lyons, where we were handed over to a French woman who spoke fairly good

English and who housed us for approx five weeks. Sgt Leslie D. and Sgt Joyce R. of our crew and F/O Hemmons D. [sic] from 5 Group were already there. About a fortnight after reaching this hideout we were visited by a man from Paris, name unknown, who discussed with us the possibilities of getting us home. He gave us to understand that he might be able to arrange for an aircraft to fetch us, if we could find a suitable landing place in the vicinity. This man visited us on four different occasions and on his last visit at the end of Jul matters had got so far that we had found a suitable landing strip and were awaiting news as to when the aircraft would turn up. However, at the beginning of Aug the local resistance came to fetch us, telling us that they were going to fly us home.

Right
Commemorative plaque to Huguette Verhague; plaque marking the crash site of Philip Hemmens's No.49 Squadron Lancaster and recording his death at Buchenwald on 18 October 1944.
Jeff Boyling

The French woman who had risked her life to shelter the five airmen was Huguette Verhague, who would later be afforded the accolade heroine of the Resistance for her selfless actions. Don Leslie's introduction to her came about after his landing by parachute, when he heard a dog bark and followed the sound until he chanced across her modest farmhouse in the nearby village of Mortemer. On first seeing Don he recalled 'she was scared to death', but she disappeared into her house and emerged with bread, a half-bottle of wine and a note from Reg Joyce. Though terrified that she'd be discovered by German soldiers, Huguette offered the airmen shelter in her barn, where they remained hidden for six weeks. In his IS9 report Don included Huguette's home address and proclaimed: 'She should be cited for a Decoration

for all she did for us.'

The five evaders, including Flying Officer Hemmens (who had sustained a broken arm when his Lancaster crashed), were now in the care of the local French Resistance, part of the 'Comet Line' network that helped Allied evaders to escape south through occupied France into neutral Spain and home via British-controlled Gibraltar. However, what the Resistance was unaware of at this time was that the escape line had been infiltrated by Jacques Desoubrie, a traitor and double agent of Belgian descent, who worked for the Gestapo during the German occupation of France. Desoubrie, who used various aliases during his treacherous career but preferred to be known as 'Captain Jacques', was personally responsible for the capture of many of the 168 Allied airmen who in August 1944 would be transported to Buchenwald concentration camp.

In his IS9 statement Arthur Eagle details the series of events surrounding the total deception and betrayal that he and his fellow evaders suffered, so masterfully orchestrated by the traitorous Desoubrie:

They took us in a car to Heuqeville [sic], about 5 miles from the river Seine and about 10 miles North West of Les Andelys. There we were handed over to a local farmer who housed us for a day and night. During that time we were joined by 2 U.S. airmen who were supposed to fly with us. We received civilian clothes and one morning a large car turned up to fetch us. The Americans remained behind whilst the car took the remaining 5 of us into Paris, to the district of Auteuil.

We were taken to a large empty mansion in the district: there were about 3 Frenchmen waiting for us, who told us that the plan had been changed and they were going to try to get us down into Spain. For security reasons, they explained, they removed all our belongings which could possibly have been identified with England. After a meal, Hemmons [sic], Leverington and myself were taken to a small hotel near the station of Auteuil, whilst the other two went off somewhere in another party. We spent one night in the hotel where we met two American fliers and the next morning a man came for us and conducted us to two cars which were waiting nearby. These cars set off at a great rate, droce [sic] us into the centre of the town and pulled up outside the Gestapo H.Q. and that was that. We were then moved to Fresnes prison where we remained about a week.

The brief mention of their captivity in the IS9 reports does not give any indication of the conditions in which they were incarcerated or the treatment they received. The captured airmen had been labelled 'terrorflieger' (terror flyers) by the German authorities and consequently were not afforded the legal status of prisoners of war. They did not receive a trial and were initially transported to Fresnes prison on 9 or 10 August, where they would remain until 15 August. The town of Fresnes is located just south of Paris and during the war the prison was used by the Germans to house British SOE agents and members of the French Resistance, who were held in horrific conditions and subjected to torture and execution. In 1944 it was also used to hold the 168 Allied airmen, who

But one event to mention involved the young F/O Hemmens, former fellow evader of Reg and his crewmates. Hemmens, whose broken arm had only received cursory treatment and binding by his captors, was only rescued from an imminent beating by a sadistic baton-wielding SS guard due to the swift intervention of the senior Allied officer and New Zealander, Squadron Leader Philip Lamason, who confronted a senior guard and demanded that his subordinate be ordered to stop his indiscriminate lashing out at the airmen. Thankfully, the senior guard eventually heeded the request and approached the red-faced thug, who after some stern words low-

Left Noel Pardon's grave; Nigel Campbell's grave; Jack Wilson's grave. *Jeff Boyling*

would later be transferred en masse to Buchenwald concentration camp, just five days before Paris was liberated by British and American forces. The airmen would not be immune to the brutal beatings or constant threats of death at Fresnes, and as a permanent legacy of his short spell there, Don Leslie would lose two front teeth at the hands of his captors.

With the Allies rapidly advancing on Paris, the evacuation of the airmen commenced on 15 August 1944, when they were shuttled by a series of buses to the city's Gare de l'Est station and loaded into boxcars at the nearby Pantin freight yards. The five-day journey undertaken in those boxcars was one of danger, suffering and brutality; however, space precludes the retelling of the various episodes in any great detail.

ered his baton. A small victory and temporary respite for the injured Hemmens, who tragically was not destined to survive the maltreatment and misery so synonymous with the hell that was Buchenwald.

The next phase of incarceration for Reg and his fellow airmen is a perfect illustration of how man's inhumanity towards his fellow man can manifest itself in times of war, whereby ever greater depths of moral depravity are readily achieved. Notwithstanding the passing of almost seven decades since the last world war, the horror of the Nazi death camps that resulted in the Holocaust and the mass murder of the Romanies and those with disabilities, still remains fresh in much of the world's psyche. What is not necessarily common knowledge, though, is that these camps also held many other categories of prisoner, including for a two-month period in 1944, 168 Allied airmen who had each been branded 'terrorflieger' and falsely classed as criminals, thereby forfeiting their right to POW status in accordance with the Geneva Convention. Illegally imprisoned in Buchenwald concentration camp, the airmen would, as well as their own sufferings, bear witness to the inhuman treatment meted out to the skeletal inmates who populated the main camp, from which they were segregated. It is therefore not surprising that it was never going to be in the interests of the German authorities to release these men, and surviving official documents were clearly annotated to the effect that the airmen were not to be transferred to another camp. Their fate was effectively sealed.

The 168 airmen, comprising a broad spectrum of nationalities from the air forces of Britain, the Commonwealth and the USA, eventually arrived at Buchenwald on 20 August 1944, and hereafter Reg became prisoner No. 78401. Suffice it to say they did not receive a warm welcome and the new arrivals were shocked to hear the crackling sounds emanating from the electric fence as they entered the camp, plus witness the sight of smoke belching from the chimney of a building soon to be identified as the crematoria. Sinisterly, some of the new arrivals were mockingly informed by a guard that the only way they would leave the camp would be up through the chimney. The aircrew would bear witness to the horrifying reality of life behind the wire of Buchenwald, and the toll that such treatment inevitably took on the fragility of human existence.

The airmen first had all hair roughly sheared from their heads and bodies by Russian prisoners, and while still bleeding from multiple nicks they were then ushered into a shower block, where many feared they might be entering a gas chamber. These fears were unfounded, fortunately, and each prisoner was then issued with second-hand prison garb of cotton shirt, trousers and cap. There were to be no shoes issued and thereafter they remained bare-footed. The men were not housed with the other inmates in the main camp of Buchenwald, but were instead sent to live in a fenced area known as the 'Little Camp'. For the first three weeks there was no accommodation for the prisoners, except some tents for housing the seriously sick only, so they had no option but to sleep in the open and on the cobbled surface. Salvation at this

point was to come from some Russian POWs, who gave up a number of blankets to the newcomers. Each blanket had to be shared by five airmen and the most valued position for sleep was in the middle of the group, where maximum warmth was provided. The inmates were eventually found a lice-infested room in the barracks, which undoubtedly prevented many deaths from hypothermia or any of the other prevalent diseases that plagued them. Their staple diet was potato peel, but again the Russians gave up some of their scraps, despite their own states of near starvation.

Around mid-October Phil Lamason got wind from reliable sources that specific orders had been received from Berlin, stating that all of the Allied airmen, including the bedridden and desperately ill, were to be exterminated within the week, a fact that he chose to keep to himself rather than cause panic. To stave off any such eventuality, influential inmates within the camp swiftly arranged for a message to be smuggled out of the camp by an outside working party at the nearby Luftwaffe airfield, with a request that an officer pass this information to the Luftwaffe hierarchy in Berlin. The plan was obviously successful, as none other than an outraged Herman Goering came to the aid of the airmen and obtained their immediate transfer to Luftwaffe control. The lives of 166 of the Allied aircrew had been saved. Unfortunately, for two of the original 168 salvation had come too late. On 27 September 1944, F/O Philip Derek Hemmens succumbed to septicaemia caused by the cuts on his feet, rheumatic fever and pneumonia. He was twenty years old. The treatment he had received in the camp hospital was nothing short of barbaric, where his joints had been opened up with a knife. He was cremated and is today listed among the missing on the Runnymede Memorial, his date of death being recorded as 18 October 1944. The other fatality was a USAAF fighter pilot, who had to remain at Buchenwald due to severe illness and died on 29 November 1944.

Reg and thirty of his fellow NCO airmen, including his three crewmates, arrived at the North Compound of Stalag Luft III from Buchenwald on 21 October 1944. He had become POW No. 8100 and was now subject to treatment as per the articles of the Geneva Convention. The North Compound was designated for officers only, but when the other NCOs were eventually transferred out, Reg managed to secure himself a permanent attachment to the camp, by carrying out menial duties such as sweeping floors. It was also while in the camp that he received notification that he had been promoted to flight sergeant. As the war drew to a close Reg, Ron, Arthur and Don, having taken part in various forced marches owing to the advances of the Russians, were finally liberated. Reg eventually regained freedom on 9 May 1945, the day after VE Day. An Allied officer and soldier suddenly arrived in a jeep and the commandant of the prisoners, at that time a German naval officer, handed over his pistol to the officer by way of surrender. Reg was then taken to an airfield in Holland, where he spent the night in an Avro Anson, which was missing a wheel and meant that he slept on a precarious slant. The next day Reg became a beneficiary of Operation Exodus, when he was flown back to the UK in an Avro Lancaster, part of an all-out effort implemented by Bomber Command to repatriate Allied POWs to Britain.

Ron Leverington, Don Leslie and Arthur Eagle were eventually liberated by Russian forces at Stalag Luft III A, Luckenwalde, on 22 April 1945. On 8 May, Ron and Don, along with fellow RAF airmen, Flight Sergeants Harper and Bauram, were walking outside the camp when an American jeep came along the road. The driver told the four men there was a convoy of trucks about a mile down the road, so they walked on until they found them, and one took them

on to Barby. From Barby they travelled by road to Heidelsheim and flew from there to Brussels. They entrained at Brussels for Lille and boarded a plane back to the UK, arriving on 14 May.

After the war Reg remained in the RAF, remustering on 26 November 1945 as a personnel administration clerk. After a series of postings within the UK he was transferred to France on 26 August 1946, where he remained up until his release from the service in February 1947. By some chance, when visiting the crash site of LW143 and the local area of Lyons-la-Forêt, Reg happened across a young lady by her garden gate, who turned out to be Janine Colzy, the young girl who had witnessed his parachute descent in 1944. The meeting proved fateful, as Reg and Janine were later married, on 16 July 1949, in her home village of Lyons-la-Forêt, just over five years from the day that Reg was blown from the rear turret of LW143. With this marriage came yet another twist to the tale, this time regarding Janine's father, Gustave Colzy, who had been a radio operator in the local French Resistance when Reg was shot down. In 1944 Gustave had also suffered capture by the Germans and incarceration in Buchenwald, where his stay coincidentally overlapped that of Reg's. He too would witness the horrors of the death camp and, against the odds, live to see the uniting of his beloved daughter with one of the many airmen who had received the courageous assistance of his former resistance movement. ●

Left Jack Wilson's medals. *Peter Cook*

CHAPTER TEN

NOT FORGOTTEN

BY STEVE DARLOW

AMID THE SUNFLOWERS, CHRIS BEARE, THE NIECE OF BOMBER COMMAND NAVIGATOR DENNIS BLUMFIELD, REACHED DOWN AND PICKED UP A SMALL PIECE OF LANCASTER WRECKAGE AND TURNED IT OVER IN HER HAND. SIXTY YEARS PREVIOUSLY, HER UNCLE HAD LOST HIS LIFE WHERE SHE WAS NOW STANDING. THE FIELD HAD NOT BEEN CULTIVATED, SUCH WAS THE RESPECT OF THE LOCAL FRENCH PEOPLE, BELIEVING THE AREA MAY STILL HOLD THE REMAINS OF SOME OF THE AIRCREW. THERE WERE ONLY SUNFLOWERS, BOWING THEIR HEADS IN THE AFTERNOON SUN.

EARLIER CHRIS, with her brother, son and daughter, had visited the graves of the entire crew of Lancaster ND684 of No. 49 Squadron. They had met an elderly gentleman who fought back tears as he recalled the tragic night back in July 1944. He had collected pieces of Window and crafted them into rings for girls in the neighbourhood. They met the local lady who tended the graves and ensured the young Bomber Command airmen's final resting place was regularly refreshed with newly cut flowers. They toasted the crew and new friendships in the local Mairie, and then set off for the crash site. As Chris recalled: 'We were invited to wander up and down the rows of sunflowers. Words cannot express the emotion we felt. There were small pieces of plane wreckage on the ground and we collected a few pieces. It was surreal and I kept saying "It's 60 years today that my uncle died here. I can't believe that although I never met him, I am standing here and collecting pieces of wreckage from his plane."'

Through the early months of 1944 Dennis Blumfield passed through the various standard training units as he prepared for operations and progressed from sergeant to flight sergeant. He kept up a fairly regular correspondence with his mother Margaret Blumfield. On 15 February, writing from RAF Wigsley, he told her of his new pilot, Australian Bill Appleyard: 'I hope you are quite well by now. I am still in the best of health and enjoying life. We have started flying. Our crew was the first to go solo. Bill is certainly a wizard pilot. I think he is definitely the best on the course.' On 5 March 1944 Dennis again wrote to his mother. He was nearing the end of his training, along with some of his future operational colleagues, one of whom, Geoff Perry, was particularly happy: 'Geoff's wife had her baby on March 1st. It's a girl. He's very impressed because it weighs $9^1/_2$ lbs. He has been going around with a stupid grin on his face ever since.' Dennis also reported that he was not too enamoured with their current station, RAF Wigsley: 'I am not doing too well on this course at the moment. I am again scared of being thrown off. … This is still a pretty foul place; not very much consideration for the men. The conditions cannot be helped but keenness on keeping in step could beneficially be replaced by efforts in keeping the morale high.' Twelve days later Dennis's letter was more optimistic:

1393228
F/Sgt Blumfield
Sgts' Mess
RAF Station Syerston
Notts
17 March 1944

Dear Mum
As you already know, we have been moved. We are now on the second day of an eighteen day course. Afterwards we get posted to a squadron. I hope you are not the silly kind who worries. Remember that the losses are getting less every time. We have a far better chance now, than we would have had a year ago. … This station is a vast improvement on Wigsley. Wigsley was the worst station I have ever been on. We are six miles from Newark and fourteen from Nottingham. The latter is a pretty good place for entertainment. …
Love Dennis
PS I cannot get the allotment settled for another week or two.
PPS Where's my laundry?

Left Dennis Blumfield.
Elsie Holwill née Blumfield

On 6 April Dennis wrote to 'Dear Mum' from RAF Fiskerton and informed her of his new squadron: 'We were posted here today from Syerston. This place is comparatively new but from all accounts it seems to be a bang on place. The squadron number is forty nine. Thank you for all the good wishes. This is one of the best squadrons. …' As there is no mention, one assumes Dennis had received his laundry by then. Starting on the night of 18/19 April with an attack on the Juvisy rail centre, and through April and May 1944, Dennis Blumfield's crew, with Australian Bill Appleyard at the controls, played their part in the build-up to D-Day as they attacked railyards, an air-

operation to Brunswick; and some evasive action just after bombing Morsalines coastal battery on 27/28 May. On the last night of May they were sent to the gun battery at Maisy, part of a sixty-eight-Lancaster 5 Group attack, although the operation was abandoned. Their squadron diary entry recorded: 'Seemed hopeless at first but appeared to clear before we saw the flares go down. Could not understand reason for cancelling.'

On the night of 2/3 June the crew's involvement in the Allied deception plan was frustrated when a large force attacked coastal gun emplacements in the Pas-de-Calais area, attempting to deceive the Germans

Right Chris Beare, niece of Bomber Command navigator Dennis Blumfield.
Elsie Holwill née Blumfield

craft factory, a coastal gun battery and the German tank depot at Mailly-le-Camp, in addition to a minelaying operation and raids to German targets and Oslo. Their squadron diary entries for the period are fairly standard, with the occasional sentence noting anything the crew deemed worthy of special mention: 'Fires could be seen for 100 miles on return', in respect of the 28/29 April raid to the airframe works at Oslo; 'Three big explosions very outstanding', referring to the 1/2 May raid to the aircraft works at Toulouse; 'Coming home we deviated North to avoid a belt of searchlights', in regard to the 22/23 May

as to the true whereabouts of the beach landings. Prior to Pilot Officer Bill Appleyard's crew dropping their bombload, the order to cease bombing came through. But on the eve of D-Day they would be blasting enemy positions, attacking the gun battery at La Pernelle, the bombload falling from 9,200 feet: 'Bombed centre of three Red and Green TIs, which were well concentrated. Bomb Aimer says he saw our stick of bombs hit the markers. Quite a good trip.' Following a landing at 0534 hours their Lancaster ND684 was prepared for another raid that night, the crew taking off at 0040 hours to attack enemy communications in Caen.

Two nights later and No. 49 Squadron crews and Lancasters were called in to prevent enemy re-inforcement as the Allies sought to expand the beach-heads. A number of railyards had been identified, including Pontabault, which was bombed by Bill Appleyard's crew at 0051 hours: 'Bombed 2 Red Spots which H2S confirmed. Just about to bomb when the order cease bombing received so had to orbit for another run up. This spoilt trip as far as I'm concerned.'

Dennis Blumfield's direct involvement in the Normandy tactical battle is recorded in his logbook

recording 'Little if no enemy activity made it quite a straightforward trip' – and Pommeréval (24/25 June), between which they took part in the large strike on the synthetic oil works at Wesseling on 21/22 June: 'A lot of heavy flak over target. A lot of enemy activity en route in but little coming out.'

Into July and Dennis is able to note a particularly important raid in his logbook, on the caves at Saint-Leu-d'Esserent – a major V1 depot – although the cost was high, with thirty-one aircraft lost. The entry in the squadron diary against Bill Appleyard's Lancaster ND684 records: '4908N 0155E at 0107 hrs at 13,500 ft, flying bomb seen launched roughly on

Left Dennis Blumfield, back row, third from the left, '63 Course Nav'. *Elsie Holwill née Blumfield*

in respect of his next three raids, to Étampes on 9 June, Caen on 12 June, and Aunay-sur-Odon on 14 June. Again there was little opposition, and Dennis had been keen to report that fact to his mother Margaret in a letter of 12 June: 'Sorry I am a little over-due in writing. We have been quite busy just lately 27, 31, 2, 5, 6, & 9. We have now done sixteen. Everybody in the crew is OK and as usual we just fly out & back and nobody seems to take a lot of notice to us.' Then came a shift in the nature of their tar-gets when the crew attacked the V-weapon sites at Beauvoir (16/17 June) – their squadron diary entry

reciprocal from position almost below our aircraft, but slightly on port bow.' The crew's next operational experience took them to the railyards at Culmont on 12/13 July, reported as a successful attack: 'Number of bomb bursts all well concentrated around markers. Route trouble free and well planned.' Similarly, their following sortie into enemy airspace would be 'well planned'. Indeed, the air chiefs had been keen to take out this particular target for some time and had worked on the operational requirements according-ly. But attempts to avoid the airborne enemy failed that night. The next squadron diary entry against

Right Sergeant Everett Matheson (RCAF) – air gunner. Below Sergeant Geoffrey Perry – wireless operator.
Elsie Holwill née Blumfield

Lancaster ND684, piloted by Bill Appleyard with Dennis Blumfield as navigator, was testament to the fact that this raid had not been 'trouble free', simply recording 'Missing without trace.'

Since the day of the invasion the tactical air plan was discussed at a daily meeting of the Allied air commanders, which began with an appreciation of the weather conditions followed by a summary of the enemy troop movements. At the thirty-eighth meeting on 8 July the air chiefs were briefed on military movements as identified by Allied reconnaissance, with the main activity seen on the rail lines Saarbrücken–Vitry and Belfort–Wesoul–Dijon. At the conclusion of the meeting Bomber Command was tasked to attack Revigny, east of Vitry. In fact, Revigny would feature regularly over the course of the next ten days in respect of priorities allocated to Bomber Command. But so would V-weapon targets, which would actually prove to be the main targets until 12 July.

But Air Chief Marshal Sir Trafford Leigh Mallory, commanding the Allied Expeditionary Air Force, was keen for a return to attacking rail targets, bolstered by the fact that there was a general belief that reinforcements would be coming into the battle area following the dismissal of their adversary Field Marshal Gerd von Rundstedt and the appointment of Field Marshal Günther von Kluge as Commander-in-Chief West.

On Tuesday 11 July Leigh Mallory voiced his opinion on the success of the railway plan and that it was clear that the Germans were using Paris as a main unloading and distribution centre and strikes should be launched on Vaires, Noisy-le-Sec and Villeneuve-Saint-Georges. 'Attacks on these places would achieve a double object of smashing up whatever rolling stock, supplies etc., were there at the time and also of throwing the supply system out of joint for the future.'

Bomber Command's Commander-in-Chief Air Chief Marshal Sir Arthur Harris questioned the value of continuing raids. They had been attacking since April, 'and as far as he could see they might go on forever without achieving any decisive result'. He believed the cost had been too heavy and that Bomber Command's casualties since April had been almost equal to those of the British Army in

Normandy. Leigh Mallory was insistent that the assaults would 'pay dividend'. Harris remained unmoved when it came to attacks on marshalling yards. Deputy Supreme Allied Commander Air Chief Marshal Sir Arthur Tedder settled the debate: 'The Allies had established and held a bridgehead in Normandy … all reports went to show that a great deal had been achieved in the way of actual destruction of stores and marshalling yards.'

The railyards at Revigny remained in the targeting priorities and on the night of 12/13 July Bomber Command's 1 Group attacked, but the raid was seriously hampered by cloud, and ten Lancasters were lost. Indeed, the raid on 14/15 July had to be aborted as the railyards could not be clearly identified, at a cost of seven Lancasters. Despite the frustration the call on Bomber Command to block the rail supply route through Revigny remained. At the Allied Air Commanders' Conference on 16 July Military Intelligence was still reporting substantial rail traffic and Revigny was prioritised. As an aside it is interesting to note Sir Arthur Harris's comment at the meeting: 'Air Chief Marshal Harris said that there was considerable discontent in his Command owing to the continued ban on leave; his Command had been fighting the War for three years, and he could not see why leave should be stopped now just because the Army had started.' But it appears that the weather again prevented an operation that night, and V-weapon sites were attacked the next day.

On the morning of 18 July Bomber Command directly intervened in the land battle, dropping approximately 5,000 tons on targets in support of Operation Goodwood. Sir Arthur Harris also mentioned that that night they were 'laying on operations against marshalling yards at Vaires, Aulnoye and Revigny'. The following day Leigh Mallory expressed his appreciation of the efforts that night, the minutes of the AAC meeting recording 'that railways to South and East of Paris now appeared to be fairly quiet. This might be expected after recent attacks on Nevers, Culmont and Chalons-Sur-Marne, and yesterday's attacks on Revigny, Strasbourg, and Saarbrücken. The main movement appeared to be now in Northern France, but he did not think that at the moment there were any targets here for Bomber Command.' Success could be claimed, but Bomber Command airmen had died hindering German reinforcement.

Left Pilot Officer William (Bill) Appleyard (RAAF) – Pilot. Below Flight Sergeant George Jameson – air bomber.
Elsie Holwill née Blumfield

Right Sergeant Robert (Bob) Viollet – air gunner. Below Sergeant Howard Turner – flight engineer.
Elsie Holwill née Blumfield

On the afternoon of 18 July 1944 the crew of Lancaster III ND684, EA-V prepared themselves for their twenty-sixth operational sortie. That night navigator Dennis Blumfield, Australian pilot Bill Appleyard, flight engineer Howard Turner, bomb aimer George Jameson, wireless operator Geoffrey Perry, Canadian air gunner Everett Matheson and air gunner Bob Viollet would be going to the marshalling yards at Revigny, taking off at 2249 hours. They were an experienced crew and their operations to date had been quite diverse in nature, and through a combination of skill and luck they had avoided any serious confrontations with enemy fighters. This night, however, there would be an encounter – a fatal one – and there would be no survivors to provide an account of the incident, Dennis Blumfield's Lancaster coming to ground near the village of Granges-sur-Aube in the Champagne–Ardennes region of north-eastern France. Prowling German night fighters had found the bomber stream that night and taken their toll. Fred Whitfield, DFM, flew as a rear gunner with No. 9 Squadron and recorded in his diary his recollection of the raid: 'It has to be one of the worst I've ever experienced and ever wish to encounter again. … It appeared that aircraft were going down in flames in all directions.' No. 49 Squadron would lose four aircraft that night and the crews that returned gave an insight into the aerial melee that had developed over France:

Lancaster JB399: 'A lot of fighter activity especially en route to targets.'
Lancaster PB250: 'We bombed after making four orbits to port.'
Lancaster LM190: 'Marked fighter activity, Gunners exceptionally "on their toes".'
Lancaster ND647: 'Had to wait for 12 minutes for our attack after being told to bomb.'
Lancaster ME787: 'Attacked by Ju88 4 minutes after target. Gunners returned fire and fighter broke off.'

In total Bomber Command lost 24 aircraft on the raid to Revigny, 129 airmen lost their lives, 11 were captured and there were 29 evaders. Telegrams and letters were quickly dispatched to the next of kin, leading to grief, shock, uncertainty, hope, anxiety – and ultimately relief or despair. For the next of kin of the crew of Lancaster ND684 it was to be despair.

Date	Hour	Aircraft Type and No	Pilot	Duty	Remarks (including results of bombing, gunnery exercises, etc.)	Flying Times Day	Night
					Time carried forward :	185·15	101·10
1·5·44	21·50	LANCASTER' P/O	Appleyard	Navigator	Ops. TOLOUSE		7·45
3·5·44	12·50	V	P/o Appleyard	Navigator	N.F.T.	00·30	
3·5·44	22·00	V	P/o Appleyard	Navigator	Ops. MAILLY		5·40
15·5·44	17·05	V	P/o Appleyard	Navigator	Air Sea Firing	00·45	
15·5·44	20·35	R	P/o Appleyard	Navigator	Bombing	1·25	
17·5·44	11·10	V	P/o Appleyard	Navigator	Bombing (Bomb sight U.S.)	00·20	
17·5·44	15·10	V	P/o Appleyard	Navigator	Low level + bombing (Early return weather)	00·50	
18·5·44	12·15	V	P/o Appleyard	Navigator	Test	00·55	
19·5·44	11·20	V	P/o Appleyard	Navigator	N.F.T.	00·40	
19·5·44	23·15	V	P/o Appleyard	Navigator	OPS AMIENS		3·55
21·5·44	14·20	V	P/o Appleyard	Navigator	N.F.T.	00·20	
21·5·44	22·50	V	P/o Appleyard	Navigator	OPS KIEL BAY (Gardening)		6·30
22·5·44	22·05	V	P/o Appleyard	Navigator	OPS BRUNSWICK		6·20
24·5·44	14·30	V	P/o Appleyard	Navigator	H.L.B (Record) Fighter Affil.	1·50	
27·5·44	14·10	V	P/o Appleyard	Navigator	N.F.T.	0·40	
27·5·44	23·05	V	P/o Appleyard	Navigator	OPS MORSALINES		3·20
28·5·44	16·00	V	P/o Appleyard	Navigator	H.L.B	1·30	
29·5·44	12·50	V	P/o Appleyard	Navigator	Special Training	1·25	
30·5·44	14·40	V	P/o Appleyard	Navigator	N.F.T	0·25	
31·5·44	12·45	V	P/o Appleyard	Navigator	N.F.T	0·20	
					Total Time ·	197·40	134·40

Left
Dennis Blumfield's logbook showing all operations throughout May, 1944.' *Chris Beare*

At first seven families had to contend with the uncertainty surrounding the crew's fate. Numerous letters were exchanged and excerpts from those written by Nellie Jameson to Dennis Blumfield's mother, Margaret, are typical of the content:

....

29 October 1944
Dear Mrs Blumfield
Just a few lines to know if you have had any news of Dennis yet, or if any of the others have had any news. We have not heard anything of George, it does seem such a long time this waiting and wondering where they are. I suppose you have not heard from the parents of the Canadian and Australian.

One thing one reads many cases of airmen returning home so we must hope that it will not be long before our boys return.

....

12 November 1944
Dear Mrs Blumfield,
Thank you very much for your letter. We were very sorry to

hear the news about the Canadian, it must have been a terrible shock for his folks. Will you let me have his Mothers address for I should like to write to her.

I wrote to Mrs Bartlett, Mrs Perry & Mr Viollet last week to see if they had heard any news. I have not heard from Mrs Perry yet but the other two had no news. Mr Viollets letter has certainly given us a little more hope. His other son that was missing on May 3rd turned up at home on Aug 24th, he is the only one that got back because he kept on walking, the others were taken prisoner. He says he is sure we shall have some good tidings of them soon.

....

3 March 1945
Dear Mrs Blumfield,
Just a few lines to know if you have heard anymore news yet. When they sent us the news about E.M. Matheson and the other three unidentified we sent back and asked if they could tell us where they came down and where they were buried. At the time they could give us no news, but today we had a letter from the Air Ministry saying that a further report has now been received from the International Red Cross

**Right
Dennis Blumfield's
logbook showing
operations from
1 to 16 June, 1944.'**
Chris Beare

Committee, Geneva, which states that Sergeant E.M.
Matheson, and the three unidentified airmen were buried in
the cemetery at Granges-sur-Aube, approximately 47 miles
south of Reims. They regret that is it still not possible to
state precisely who are the three unidentified.

I don't know if you have received this report but I felt sure
in case you had not that you would like to know. We keep
hopeing [sic] that now the Russians have freed a lot of our
men that we might hear some fresh news.

One thing it is nice to know is that to whoever the poor
lads belong they have at least been buried properly. I hope it
will not be long now before we get some definite news for it is
now nearly 8 months.

....

11 March 1945
Dear Mrs Blumfield,
Thank you very much for the photo and your letter. It certainly
would be very nice to have a photo of all the crew. We
haven't a spare photo of George at present but am having
some copied from the one we have got and then will let you
have one.

I was so pleased to hear you had been to the Air Ministry,
as you say it does seem funny that three of them should go up
without their discs on. I think the same as you do, that the
Germans looked at one disc, just for identification purposes,
and never bothered about the other three, for it is just the sort
of thing they would do.

I have said all along that I thought your son and George
were the first two to bail out if anything happened to the
plane, it certainly gives us a wee bit more hope. As you say
we must be patient and hope for news soon. Perhaps it won't
be long now that so many prisoners are now being released.

....

28 May 1945
Dear Mrs Blumfield,
We have heard no news yet, have you heard anything. We did
think that now the war had finished we would have heard
something, didn't you. I had a letter a few weeks back from
Mrs Perry and she had not heard anything. We are going to
write to the Red Cross again and see if they can give us
any news. If I hear anything I will let you know.

....

Left
Dennis Blumfield's
logbook showing
operations from
18 to 24 June, 1944.'
Chris Beare

Over time, with the help of onlookers who were able to describe the realities of the air war, the families were finally able to gather details of the circumstances in which their relative died. A few weeks following the end of the war in Europe the family of Sergeant Viollet received a letter from an eyewitness.

....

Department De La Marne Grange

Arrondissement D'Epernay

Canton D'Anglure

Grange-Sur-Aube

27 May 1945

Sir, In answer to your letter of 19th May, I have the honour to provide the following information. After the fall of Sergeant Viollet's machine I immediately went to the scene of the accident. I belonged to the Resistance and, despite the danger of unexploded bombs, I wanted to prevent the Germans getting the airmen's documents and personal objects.

Sergeant Viollet was the only man recognisable. He was still at his post, at his guns. His hand was bandaged, having probably lost a finger. He also had a few wounds to his face,

and we found out at his burial that both of his legs were fractured. I was able to take his identity disc, some money and a French map which he was carrying. The Germans then gave us the order to take away the corpses and bury them. Despite the occupation, we gave him and his companions a moving service in which all the population took part. Your comrade was placed alone in a plank coffin, and his belongings were put in with him. Two other coffins were placed near his containing the rest of the non-identified airmen.

You can feel reassured in respect of the grave, that it is carefully looked after by the borough and all the population makes it their duty to respectfully lay flowers. I am unable for the moment to let you have a photograph of the grave, film being unobtainable, but I will do my best as soon as possible. I add, to end, that the personal objects have been collected by a Lieutenant Kenneth, Commandant of the Military Cemetery at Champigneul (Marne), this officer having come and taken all the information relating to that crew.

I pray you to believe, Sir, the expression of my distinguished sentiments.

The Mayor

....

Right
Dennis Blumfield's logbook showing his final entries.
Chris Beare

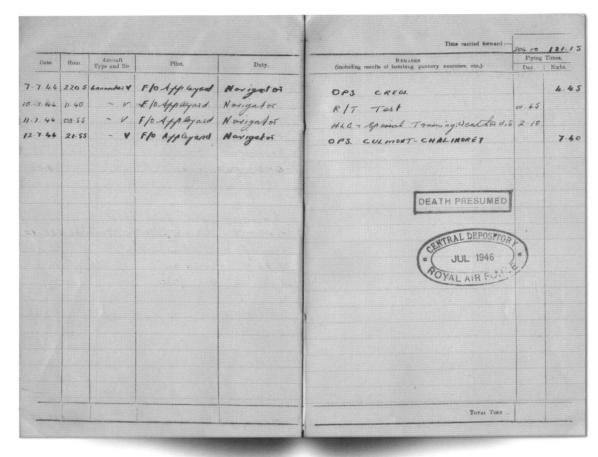

Date	Hour	Aircraft Type and No	Pilot.	Duty.	Remarks (including results of bombing, gunnery exercises, etc.)	Day.	Night.
					Time carried forward :— 204.00 181.15		
7.7.44	22.05	Lancaster V	F/O Appleyard	Navigator	OPS CREW		4.45
10.7.44	11.40	~ V	F/O Appleyard	Navigator	R/T Test	0.45	
11.7.44	08.55	~ V	F/O Appleyard	Navigator	H.L.B. → Special Training: Weather U.S	2.10	
12.7.44	21.55	~ V	F/O Appleyard	Navigator	OPS. CULMONT-CHALINDREY		7.40

DEATH PRESUMED

CENTRAL DEPOSITORY
JUL 1946
ROYAL AIR FORCE

TOTAL TIME .

On 20 November 1945 the mayor of Granges-sur-Aube wrote to Margaret Blumfield:

....

Dear Madame,
In response to your letter of the 3rd November I have the honour to inform you that the plane in which your son was flying was in flames before it fell. The disabled machine had lost many parts – the tail, wing, and engine, and was out of control. Sergeant Viollet was found inside his turret some 250yds from where the aircraft fell, thus we were able to identify him. Another body was found about 20 yards away badly charred and carried the inscription 'Canada' on the shoulder of the flying jacket.

As for the other members of the crew, it was unfortunately impossible to identify them; they were too badly disfigured by the exploding bombs still in the plane. Their remains have been placed in a communal grave. Such belongings as we were able to collect were handed to the military authorities (civil establishment).

I have just had a visit by British Air Force Officers who came to honour and salute at the grave, and take a photograph, one of which will be sent to you. In addition they also collected all the information concerning the fall of the aircraft.

The population here make it their duty, always, to care for the grave and place flowers when possible. Although they are far from you, they are not forgotten or abandoned. I beg you to believe, Madame, my assurance of our respectful sympathy.
The Mayor

....

To the list of Bomber Command airmen's names, that record the individuals who were sacrificed for the liberation of France from Nazi occupation, could be added those of the crew of a No. 49 Squadron four-engine Avro Lancaster bomber, serial number ND684: 21-year-old Dennis Blumfield, 22-year-old Bill Appleyard, 24-year-old Howard Turner, 31-year-old George Jameson, 21-year-old Geoffrey Perry, 21-year-old Everett Matheson and 24-year-old Bob Viollet rest, and are commemorated with Commonwealth War Graves Commission headstones, in the Granges-sur-Aube churchyard. ●

Left Granges-sur-Aube churchyard. Left to right: Dennis Holwill, Chris Beare, Marianne Beare and Peter Beare.
Chris Beare

Right
Chris Beare, amid the sunflowers.
Elsie Holwill née Blumfield

CHAPTER ELEVEN

A LONELY PLACE TO BE

BY ANDREW MACDONALD

STUTTGART WAS A WORLD AWAY FROM THE YORKSHIRE WOLDS. IN ONE OF THE MANY DOZENS OF WARTIME AIRFIELDS NOW SCATTERED ACROSS THE NORTH OF ENGLAND, NINETY-ONE TIRED AND ANXIOUS-LOOKING YOUNG MEN STARED ACROSS THE BRIEFING ROOM AT A GIANT MAP OF EUROPE. THEIR EYES FOLLOWED THE LONG LINES OF TAPES STRETCHING ACROSS FRANCE AND THEN DEEP INTO THE HEART OF GERMANY. THE DISTANCE ALONE WAS ENOUGH TO UNNERVE EVEN THE MOST EXPERIENCED AMONG THEM BUT THE 'COVENTRY OF GERMANY' WAS ALSO A DANGEROUS TARGET AS WELL. WHILE JUST AS PERILOUS IN THEIR OWN WAY, THE BOYS HAD BECOME ACCUSTOMED TO THE MUCH SHORTER OPERATIONS ACROSS THE CHANNEL IN FRANCE AND BELGIUM. MOST WERE NO MORE THAN THREE TO FOUR HOURS AT A TIME. THIS WOULD BE DOUBLE THAT AT THE VERY LEAST AND WAS A DEEP PENETRATION RAID. EVERY SINGLE SORTIE PRESENTED RISKS, BUT THE MEN REASONED LOGICALLY THAT IF THEY SPENT LESS TIME OVER OCCUPIED TERRITORY, THAT MEANT LESS TIME BEING SHOT AT AND STALKED BY GERMAN NIGHT FIGHTERS OR BEING CONED AND BLOWN TO BITS BY ANTI-AIRCRAFT GUNS.

ONCE THE squadron briefing came to a close, the tension was swept aside with the chairs and the men rose to their feet and engaged in earnest conversation. They then poured out of the briefing room and eventually made their way to the parachute stores to take temporary possession of the most vital piece of equipment they would ever need but hopefully never use. There was one young 23-year-old air gunner who made a split-second decision that night and decided to draw a different type of parachute to the one he was accustomed to. He'd never done it before and it would mean even less space in the turret that didn't have much in the first place. But as it turned out, eight hours of discomfort was a small price to pay for a second chance at life. Whether it was his destiny to survive that night or nothing more than a lucky break, he would spend the next thirty-eight years ever conscious of the fact that he had been spared when so many of his close friends and comrades had not.

Robert Henry Brewer was born in the village of

Ripley, Surrey, on 23 November 1920. In addition to carrying the hopes and expectations of a proud and loving family, he was also bestowed the same name as his father, who had distinguished himself in the regular British Army across the Empire. He also inherited the natural ability to shoot and, like his dad before him, he soon fostered an abiding and lifelong affinity for the land that surrounded him. His mother Gertrude adored her son and doted on him endlessly. Bob put up with it reluctantly, as all sons do, but he knew how important he was to her and no doubt used that fact to his advantage many times over. He went to school at St Mary's, sadly long gone now, but during its long existence, the school educated and nourished the minds of at least three generations of Brewers. Life was simple then and uncomplicated. Bob's best childhood and later lifelong friend was a lad called Peter and the two were inseparable. They did everything together, and on one memorable occasion fell foul of the local farmer when the pair were caught helping themselves to his latest crop of potatoes. On hearing the owner fast approaching, Pete dropped on his belly and disappeared from the farmer's field of view. Bob, though just as quick to follow his pal's example, forgot that his backside was attached to the rest of him and in a sea of potatoes, a saluting child's bottom presented a target too good to miss. It was a wonderful childhood, and while money was never in abundance that really didn't matter. The less a child had, the more imaginative they became.

Bob was approaching his nineteenth birthday when war was declared in September 1939 and, like every able-bodied young man, would eventually find himself in the uniform of the Army, Navy or Royal Air Force. Prior to the war he had hoped to give Navy life a go, but he was subsequently turned away on the grounds that he was too young. So, undaunted by that, he decided to try his hand at the RAF and joined up in one of the recruiting centres at Blackpool in mid-1940. His lifelong mate, Dave Johnson, was there with him and both were soon scooped up for basic training. The next two to three years of Bob's service life is a little sketchy, unfortunately. It is known that both of them ended up in North Africa sometime during 1941 or 1942 when the war in that theatre was at its height. The family have a photo tucked away somewhere of the two of them standing beneath a palm tree in khaki shorts. Just exactly what

Left Bob Brewer.
Maureen Pateman and her daughter Caroline

Right Eddie Ord.
Author's collection

they did there is uncertain, but it's quite likely that they were operating as ground crew, servicing the many different aircraft the RAF used to resist and overcome Rommel's seemingly unstoppable Afrika Corps. Since Dave was probably not fit enough to meet the strict conditions of aircrew entry, eventually their paths separated and Bob returned to the UK to take up training as an air gunner. Exactly how or when is unclear, as Bob, like so many of his generation, shared precious little of his life then and left no written memoirs or recollections behind. His family remember only what Bob let slip or, in many cases, the light-hearted moments. He chose not to dwell on the tough times, even though they were never too far from his thoughts. That was just the way he was.

Bob was the perfect air gunner in appearance and aptitude. In height he was about 5 feet 7 in, was solidly built and had a keen eye. Gaming and shooting from an early age enabled him to fine tune his natural talents. By December 1943 he had not long married Ada, a shy, pretty young thing he met back in Surrey. They fell in love quickly, as couples did in war. But to begin with she found it hard to take his moustache seriously, especially when she discovered that its impressive outline was the work of a pencil. They tied the knot in November 1943 and, barely a month later, Bob was posted to RAF Harwell in Berkshire. He now proudly wore the uniform of a sergeant air gunner.

Like a lot of airfields of the day, Harwell's function changed throughout the war. The Special Operations Executive launched clandestine operations from here for a period of time, and it was from where the first British paratroops to land on D-Day set off to make history in those peculiar-looking Horsa gliders built almost entirely of wood. Bob's time at Harwell may not have had the same dramatic impact on the course of the war, but it was certainly an important moment in his life and it was here that he would meet up with five of the six men that would become his crew. In the weeks and months ahead he would grow to understand and respect them like very few other people in his life. It was an unusual relationship and one that grew out of purpose and necessity for obvious reasons. Trust, mutual understanding and respect are the fundamentals of any relationship, but they usually take years to build. These men had a matter of months to make these bonds. How could anyone in

a situation like this be sure that they were making the right choice? Especially as many of these men were so young that they were still trying to get to grips with the finer points of human judgement. It might have been by mutual consent or no more scientific than pointing a finger at someone. At any rate, Bob either accidentally or quite consciously made the right choice and in a very short space of time he surrounded himself with an outstanding group of young men.

Sergeant Aubrey James Page was the pilot of the crew. Probably better remembered as Jim or Jimmy to family and friends, he was born in Streatham, London, in 1912 and was the last of thirteen immensely talented children. At thirty-two, he was a great deal older than the rest of the crew and one would imagine that the age difference was quite a drawcard for men almost a decade or so younger and in need of a role model. Contemporary photos depict a man of confidence, presence and charisma. He smoked a pipe, grew the almost obligatory service moustache and looked every inch the quintessential British aviator. He was also way ahead of the competition in terms of natural ability and experience, as he had flown in peacetime and, being from a family of means, piloted his own Tiger Moth. His elder sister, Connie, who lived into her one-hundredth year, remembered with some affection the summer flights she shared with her young brother at the controls. He was a gentleman pilot and his family were all incredibly proud of him.

The navigator and the second-eldest member of the crew was a fine-looking young man by the name of Ronald Marshall Simpson. He was born in Dundee, Scotland, in 1916 and had married his sweetheart Agnes in 1940. The bomb aimer, Sergeant Frederick John Court, was the eldest of three children and was born in Exeter in 1918. After attending Hele's Grammar School for boys, he joined the Metropolitan Police and was destined for great things. His family were enormously proud of him and with good reason. Then there was the mid-upper gunner, Eddie Ord. A youthful-looking young man with scarcely a line on his face, he was barely out of his teens. He came from simple working-class roots and grew up in the village of Seghill, north of Newcastle. The wireless operator, Robert Leyland, completed the early crew of six at Harwell. Like young Eddie, he too was a mere twenty years old and was born in

Right Pilot Jimmy
Page. *Bob Connell*

Preston, Lancashire. The younger boys had much in common.

Now that they had sorted themselves out as a team of six, the men had to fine tune their individual trades and further develop their relationships together on the twin-engined long-range Wellington bombers. The first stepping stone on the long path to combat was a two- to three-month course at an Operational Training Unit, where tens of thousands of crews learned to operate medium bombers in a variety of different situations, and varying degrees of appalling British weather. The hours were often long, the training intensive, and flying occurred at all hours of the day and night.

Eddie noted in his logbook their first flight at RAF Harwell on 14 January 1944. Setting off at 1430 hours, the crew flew across the cold and wintry English countryside for a cross-country exercise that lasted an hour. Jim was not the pilot in command at this stage and was probably occupying the second seat, taking instruction from a seasoned pilot now resting from operations. He would have noted the controls and handling characteristics of the old Wellington, or 'Wimpy' as she was more affectionately remembered. Ron would have had a more hands-on job as he plotted the routes to and from the airfield and ensured the aircraft did not stray from her course. It was easy to get lost as landmarks were often obscured by thick cloud, fog and numerous other prevailing weather conditions. Other exercises followed. More cross-country trips, circuits and landings, bombing and gunnery and fighter affiliations. It was the latter two that kept the gunners in the crew busy. The fighter pilots were probably nonplussed at the prospect of chasing their own bombers and having several browning machine guns trained on them. But it was a worthwhile exercise for both parties and the two gunners learned at first hand how difficult it would be to shoot a fast-moving target, especially if it was firing back at them.

By early April the crew were sent by train to the ancient city of York in the north of England. It was a city they would come to know intimately in the coming months. They disembarked there and covered the remaining nine miles south by road, until they reached the home of No. 1658 Heavy Conversion Unit. They would remain there for a month or so and would in turn learn to convert from twin-engined

aircraft to the much bigger and heavier four-engined bombers, enlarging their flying experience. Like so many hastily built airfields of the day, RAF Riccall derived its name from the neighbouring village a mile or so to the north-west. Relationships between the personnel and the villagers were perhaps a little awkward at first as the locals came to terms with the war being waged on their doorsteps. But both parties soon readily accepted one another and it was not an uncommon site to see the local pubs and village hall packed to the rafters with men and women in RAF blue. The sound of four-engined bombers overhead was now as common as the church bells on Sunday, and on 12 May Bob and his crew set off on the first of many flights in weary-looking Halifax Mark II bombers that were now well past their prime. Jim, recently promoted to the rank of pilot officer, was in the driving seat as always and there alongside him was his new flight engineer and right-hand man: 22-year-old Sergeant John Watkinson from Manchester was the latest arrival and the last man to join the already close-knit crew. Engineers were in

Left Frederick Court. *Liz O'Keeffe and Peter Willis*

many cases the quiet achievers in the crew, but rarely would you find a man with greater knowledge of the aircraft he was flying or the engines that kept them aloft. They also often enjoyed much tighter links with the ground crew because of their backgrounds.

The team of airmen took off from RAF Riccall's giant runways for the last time on 12 May 1944, exactly one month to the day they had first set off on their maiden flight in a Halifax. The total flying hours comprised 12 hours at night and some 30.35 hours in daylight. The signature of the commanding officer (Squadron Leader Williamson), acknowledged that the hours were correct and that the men were now ready to progress to an operational squadron of the Royal Air Force's choice. Since Riccall was part of 4 Group RAF, it stood to reason that the boys would remain on Halifaxes for the rest of their operational careers and no further conversion courses were needed. After their experiences with these old bangers, they were no doubt unhappy at the prospect of flying them operationally. But they needn't have worried, as they would soon take charge of brand new Halifax Mark IIIs with the much improved and reliable Bristol Hercules engines. This aircraft was a different breed entirely and for those who flew her, a new-found appreciation was soon developed for an outstanding aircraft in many respects. A few days passed and the men were probably given leave to go home and spend precious time with their families before they embarked on the most dangerous of duties. They were now an operational crew and were about to take part in one of the most strategically important periods of Bomber Command's history. Operation Overlord and the invasion of western Europe was a matter of weeks away now, although the men had very little idea of just how critical their involvement would be in the greatest seaborne invasion in history.

In mid-May, RAF Pocklington received another influx of aircrew to replace the losses of men and others who had completed their tours. Very few in fact did. No specific dates are recorded in the official squadron records but all 7 of Bob's crew are listed alongside the names of 122 other young men who presumably arrived at more or less the same time. May had been a busy month leading up to the much-anticipated invasion but, astonishingly, in four weeks only one aircraft was shot down and thankfully five

of its crew would survive. But this was just a peaceful prelude to a period of almost unprecedented loss. June would be catastrophic by comparison. No. 102 Squadron would end the war with the unfortunate distinction of suffering the third-highest level of casualties in RAF Bomber Command. Within just three months alone, approximately half of these airmen would lose their lives and another twelve of them would face the rest of the war as prisoners behind barbed wire, including Bob. Even though the Allied armies were within a whisker of invading western Europe and Germany was already struggling to fend off two very aggressive enemies on at least two fronts, she was far from beaten. There were absolutely no guarantees that any of these crews would complete their tours. It's hard to imagine how young men of twenty or twenty-one, with precious little life experience, could ever come to terms with the likelihood that they might not live long enough to see their next birthday.

On 2 June the crew found their names on the squadron Battle Order for the first time. This was it. All the long months of classroom lectures, dinghy drills, bombing, gunnery and cross-country exercises had finally brought them to this indescribable moment. It was difficult to take in. All sorts of emotions presented themselves. Tension, excitement, even relief that they were finally doing what they had been trained to do. At 1135 hours, with Bob now safely squeezed into the rear turret, the crew departed Pocklington and set off on their very first sortie to bomb Haringzelles in the Pas-de-Calais area of northern France. It was nowhere near the invasion area, but that was the whole point. In addition to removing a few gun emplacements from the map, the men also played their part in a grand deception plan to fool the Germans into believing that the invasion couldn't possibly take place in Normandy.

The dense cloud made the target difficult to see with the naked eye but it didn't prevent Fred from dropping 14,000lb of high explosives on the Germans below. They returned home safely a little after 0300 hours, and after reluctantly sitting through a debriefing, the boys finally crawled off to bed. Within the next few weeks the crew would visit many different targets with bizarre place names that were probably just as awkward to pronounce as they were to spell. Some would have passed without incident and others, like the pre-dawn raid on 6 June (which Bob flew), would have left a lasting impression on them. Very few of the aviators were even aware of the mission's significance until they returned home. Some, though, were lucky enough to see a break in the clouds and below them witnessed a naval armada the size of which had never been seen before, nor would be again. Interestingly, the targets were never revisited and that would suggest that the boys were not

the main runway at Pocklington and staggered into the night sky. Once the lead Halifax had cleared the runway safely, another would then take its place at the threshold and await the signal from the control wagon. Twelve minutes later, Jim Page received the green light to go and released the brakes of Halifax LL552. John followed the hands of his skipper and pushed the throttles forward to apply full power to all four engines. The heavy bomber rolled forward

Left Bob Brewer's logbook. *Maureen Pateman and her daughter Caroline*

only hitting their targets, but they were destroying them as well.

Unlike a lot of aircrew, Bob lived long enough to enjoy a ten-day pass after six long weeks of combat. That's how it worked. He went home to his wife and family and enjoyed what precious time he had left. He laughed, he loved and he forgot the war, which was just as well. Neither he nor his wife, of course, could anticipate that a further ten months would pass before they would see one another again. Bob had no idea that Ada was pregnant. At 2118 hours on 24 July, the first of thirteen Halifax bombers thundered down

slowly for a few seconds and then with the combined power of over 6,500 horses she began to gather tremendous speed and momentum. Only an engine failure would stop her now and John was by Jim's side ready to feather the propellers of an ailing engine should it occur. John called out the airspeed. In a short space of time the 30-ton bomber and her seven young occupants were climbing up into the darkness, oblivious of the fact that six of them had just hours to live.

There is something especially upsetting about the loss of a bomber within sight of safety and so close to home. The worst of it was far behind them surely and perhaps they could afford to relax a little now. Realistically, however, they all knew that anything could happen at any time even though they all hoped that the way home would be less problematic than being either en route to the target or over it. Even so, the gunners remained in a heightened state of readiness for hours on end, which would explain why these incredible young men were so completely exhausted at the end of each operational sortie. Bob's aircraft was so tantalisingly close, not only to the Normandy coastline but also the Allied front lines, which were a mere thirty-odd miles to the west of them. The first signs of the new dawn bathed the eastern horizon

Right Letter to Mr W. J. Court, 'I deeply regret to renew your grief'. *Liz O'Keeffe and Peter Willis*

TEL. No. Sloane 3467
HOLBORN 3494 EXT. ....

AIR MINISTRY,
ADASTRAL HOUSE,
KINGSWAY, W.C.2.

P.420655/44/S.7.Cas.C.4.

2, Seville Street,
Knightsbridge,
London S.W.1.

22 April, 1947.

Dear Mr. Court,

I deeply regret to renew your grief in the sad loss of your son, Flight Sergeant F.J. Court, but I am sure you would wish to know that a report has now been received from the Missing Research Officers in France as the result of a special investigation undertaken by them in the area of Piencourt.

The report states that the Mayor and other local residents confirm that the aircraft crashed at Piencourt and that the remains of six members of the crew were recovered from the wreckage. Unhappily owing to the severe nature of the crash it was not possible to establish the individual identity of any member. At this late stage one can only assume that Sergeant Brewer (the only survivor) was aware of the distressing condition of his dead comrades but was naturally loth to admit the circumstances to their relatives.

It was found that your son and his five comrades are interred in one grave in Piencourt Churchyard which lies about eight miles East of Lisieux. Arrangements are accordingly being made with the Graves Registration Authorities for the grave to be collectively registered and a cross erected duly inscribed with their names and service details.

May I express the hope that the knowledge of your son's last resting place may afford you some small measure of comfort in the great loss you have sustained.

Yours sincerely,

D Bent

W.J. Court, Esq.,
10, Powderham Road,
Exeter,
Devon.

with a reddish hue.

It was a minute or so after 0400 when the attack came. There was no warning or sign of any impending danger. Both gunners were completely unaware that they were being followed and that a German Bf110 night fighter, captained by Unteroffizier Helmut Burkhard, had slipped in underneath and had positioned himself perfectly for a kill. If the bomber was flying straight and level it was almost impossible to detect another aircraft beneath them. You had to weave continuously from side to side and this was tough on the captain, the controls and the fuel supply.

The forward section of the aircraft absorbed the full force of the combined cannon and machine-gun fire. The starboard wing immediately burst into flames, presumably the result of strikes on the inner fuel tanks. It may have lasted only a few seconds in reality but the attack was devastating and concentrated, unusually in the cockpit area. Bob had time to switch his microphone on and call out over the intercom. There was absolutely no word from the skipper. The only response was the intermittent sounds of Fred, who had been hit, although Bob had no idea how badly. There were few choices available to him now. If he stayed any longer, he'd certainly die. The fire was already eating its way through the wing root. The Halifax was doomed. Bob's natural instincts to survive kicked in and he turned the turret frantically with both his hands until the doors were at right angles to the fuselage, prised them open, and dropped backwards into the early morning sky. The now weakened blazing starboard wing finally gave way and folded back on itself. The aircraft was no longer controllable and she dropped from the sky like a broken sycamore seed.

There was little time to count before Bob pulled the ripcord. He was now probably only a few thousand feet above the ground before the parachute opened. The lone air gunner drifted to the ground slowly and silently, surrounded by the most exquisite early morning countryside. To the west the guns of the new Allied ground offensive opened up. They were that close – he would have heard the sounds of battle quite clearly. Not too far away the aircraft that had carried him all the way to Germany and most of the way back again, was burning furiously on the ground. It was no longer recognisable as a bomber

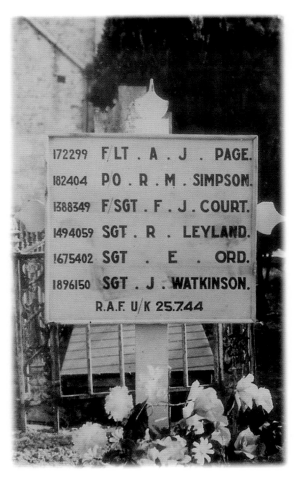

Left The crew's original burial marker.
Author's collection

and, since there were no other parachutes to be seen, it was safe to assume that only Bob had survived. He landed close to the French village of Piencourt and was most probably spirited away by the locals, who would have seen and heard the whole commotion from their homes. As was almost always the case, the French selflessly and determinedly did their very best in difficult circumstances to retrieve what remained of the airmen and bury them with dignity, treating these men as their own. The people hiding Bob also risked everything in trying to prevent him from falling into German hands. After all, he had landed right in the very middle of one of the most volatile battle zones in western Europe.

Bob was on the run for a week before he was finally captured. He was east of the River Orne when he came across a lake that looked quite enticing for a bedraggled airman on the run. So he knelt down by the water's edge to take a drink and wash his face. He noticed a group of teenagers jumping about in the water but thought nothing of it. They looked harmless enough and were too young to be of any danger. But the tomfoolery soon stopped and they started to approach him. Somehow it didn't feel right but by the time the urge came to vanish into the tree line, he soon found himself surrounded by a group of Hitler Youth. In later years Bob's family would often give him stick for being captured by a mob of German teenagers, but he was wise to give himself up. A German soldier was one thing but a gun-toting group of testosterone-infused German adolescents? That was a different matter entirely.

before he was dragged off to a prisoner of war camp in disgust.

By mid-August he had unhappily become an inmate of Stalag Luft VII, a German prisoner of war camp built in what is now modern-day Poland. All in all, it was a singularly unpleasant, boring and humiliating experience for the vast majority of inmates. Downed airmen like Bob were in effect flightless birds, and a lot of them would have felt utterly useless as the war continued to run its course irrespective of their involvement or predicament. Routines were monotonous and the days painfully

Right Funeral service of the crew, Piencourt, 1944.
Author's collection

By mid-August, Bob found himself incarcerated within the rather grim-looking walls of a Dulag Luft just outside Frankfurt. It was effectively a holding facility for Allied prisoners and was used to contain them until a more permanent location could be arranged. It was also a place of interrogation and the Germans employed all manner of elaborate methods to extract vital information from the captives. A great many prisoners were quite stunned at the extensive and accurate information the Germans actually possessed. Presumably none of this worked on Bob, who remained under the white-hot lights for only a day

long. The food, when it wasn't supplemented with Red Cross parcels, was often dreadful and it wasn't uncommon for otherwise fit and healthy young men to drop a substantial amount of weight in a short space of time. Bob was one who did and he never really recovered from the experience.

In the beginning the camp was little more than a collection of hastily prepared 'chicken huts'. They were too small for the numbers of men contained within them and were woefully inadequate on all fronts. Eventually, though, life did improve, with the construction of more permanent huts that were

**Left Bob Brewer's
Caterpillar Club
membership card.**
*Maureen Pateman and
her daughter Caroline*

forget the sight of the padre wandering up and down the ranks of prisoners in an attempt to keep their spirits up. As far as Bob was concerned men like these were the real heroes.

After the war he put his experiences to the back of his mind and instead devoted the remainder of his life to wife Ada, daughter Maureen and grandchildren Rob and Caroline. His daughter remembers him for all the right reasons. He had given her such a lovely childhood. Bob fought and lost his last battle to cancer in 1982. He never liked the idea of a big send-off, but when the day came everybody defied his wishes and turned out in huge numbers. The church was packed. It was a testament to a man who had left such a lasting impression on so many people. On that day, as the cortège stopped, Maureen looked out of the car window and there perched on a fence was an adult male pheasant, his mate and one young offspring. The usually shy birds sat perfectly still and didn't move until the car moved off. It would be interesting to know what the medium would have made of that! ●

altogether more civilised, inside and out. Bob was in hut 49, room 10, and he shared it with thirteen other airmen with similar stories to tell. They passed the long hours of each day engaged in letter writing, reading, playing sport outside in the compound and generally making as much of a nuisance of themselves as they could. They called it goon baiting. Bob had a natural flair for winding people up. On one occasion, a group of POWs got together for an impromptu seance and, as the medium probed the spirit world for likely stray souls, Bob's hands slipped under the tabletop and started delicately tapping away. He was soon booted out of the sitting, but not before the medium had told him that a daughter would be waiting for him back home. And she was.

Bob's war ended with the liberation of Luckenwalde on 20 May 1945. He was a different man when he returned but that was to be expected. He didn't sleep at all well in the early days and often paced up and down the hallways of his home in the middle of the night. Excessive noise had a jarring effect on him: he didn't like it. But when put into the context of his life at war, these disturbances are understandable. At just twenty-three, he had flown fourteen operations into France and Germany and had been shot down over Normandy. He had spent ten months behind the barbed wire of two prisoner of war camps and had endured a forced march of over 150 miles on foot and in the midst of one of the worst winters in living history. Bob never mentioned the bitter cold, the hunger or the frozen corpses by the roadside of animals and men who had lost the will to go on. He wasn't a religious man by nature, but he would never

**Left Bob Brewer
in later life.**
*Maureen Pateman and
her daughter Caroline*

"INFANTRY DIVISIONS STRUGGLING TO ARRIVE AT THE SCENE OF OPERATIONS WERE CONSTANTLY HAMPERED AND DELAYED BY ALLIED AIR ATTACKS, AND MOST OF THESE FORMATIONS HAD TO MOUNT BICYCLES OR MARCH ON THEIR FLAT FEET FOR HUNDREDS OF KILOMETRES, DUE TO THE COMPLETE DESTRUCTION OF THE RAILWAYS. MANY OF THESE TROOPS TOOK WELL OVER A WEEK BEFORE THEY PUT IN AN APPEARANCE, AND HARDLY A DIVISION ARRIVED COMPLETE, BUT RATHER STRAGGLED IN BY BITS AND PIECES".

FIELD MARSHAL GERD VON RUNSTEDT'S POST-WAR INTERROGATION.

"THE RAIDS CARRIED OUT IN RECENT WEEKS HAVE CAUSED THE BREAKDOWN OF ALL MAIN LINES; THE COASTAL DEFENCE HAVE BEEN CUT OFF FROM THE SUPPLY BASES IN THE INTERIOR, THUS PRODUCING A SITUATION WHICH THREATENS TO HAVE SERIOUS CONSEQUENCES ... LARGE SCALE STRATEGIC MOVEMENT OF GERMAN TROOPS BY RAIL IS PRACTICALLY IMPOSSIBLE".

GERMAN AIR MINISTRY REPORT, 13 JUNE 1944.

"... THE AIR OFFENSIVE AGAINST THE TRANSPORTATION BEFORE D-DAY HAD PRODUCED A STATE OF VIRTUAL PARALYSIS IN THE RAILWAY SYSTEM OF NORTHERN FRANCE AND BELGIUM. THIS WAS THE AIR'S DECISIVE CONTRIBUTION TO THAT WIDE COMPLEX OF OPERATIONS BY WHICH ALLIED MILITARY STRENGTH WAS RE-ESTABLISHED IN WESTERN EUROPE".

AIR CHIEF MARSHAL SIR ARTHUR TEDDER, DEPUTY SUPREME COMMANDER, SHAEF.

"WHOLE ARMOURED FORMATIONS, ALLOTTED TO THE COUNTER-ATTACK, WERE CAUGHT IN BOMB CARPETS OF THE GREATEST INTENSITY... THE RESULT WAS THAT THEY ARRIVED TOO LATE. THE PSYCHOLOGICAL EFFECT OF SUCH A MASS OF BOMBS COMING DOWN WITH ALL THE POWER OF ELEMENTAL NATURE UPON THE FIGHTING TROOPS... IS A FACTOR WHICH MUST BE GIVEN SERIOUS CONSIDERATION. IT IS IMMATERIAL WHETHER SUCH A BOMB CARPET CATCHES GOOD TROOPS OR BAD; THEY ARE MORE OR LESS ANNIHILATED".

FIELD MARSHAL GÜNTHER VON KLUGE, GERMAN COMMANDER-IN-CHIEF WEST, TO ADOLF HITLER 21 JULY 1944.

ACKNOWLEDGEMENTS AND NOTES

Chapter One

I would like to express my appreciation to Roger Olden for making Jack's story available, and also to Jack Forrest's daughter Ann, in particular for her help with photographs. Jack Forrest's full story is told in Mel Rolfe's book *Flying Into Hell* (Grub Street, 2001).

Chapter Two

My sincere appreciation to Alan, Ralph and Maurice Bunnagar (elder brother, youngest brother and nephew of Maurice Bunnagar), Mr John Leggitt (youngest brother of Russell Leggitt), Mrs Jean Wesson, (youngest sister of Ron Watson), Mr Nick Isfan (youngest brother of John Isfan), Mr. Tony Triesky and Mrs. Margaret Wilcoxen (Son and daughter of Cynthia Hartwell), Mr Dom Howard (researcher and historian), Mr. Rudi Stessens (aviation enthusiast and researcher).

Chapter Three

I wish to thank the following organisations and individuals for supplying photographs, information and service records of the airmen detailed in this chapter: National Archives of Canada, No. 419 Squadron Association, Frank Raeman, Ken Joyce, Didier Jadot and Theo Boiten.

Chapter Four

A special thank you to Fred and Russ Buglas. Without their help it would have not been possible to have the wonderful pictures of the crew, letters and other family stories that relate to their own relative and crew members. Also a thank you to Alexandre Bonnet from Belgium who assisted greatly in the writing of the chapter. I also wish to thank the following organisations and individuals for supplying photographs, information and service records of the airmen detailed in this chapter: National Archives of Canada, Ottawa, Theo Boiten, Ken Joyce and Didier Jadot.

Chapter Five

At least two combat reports exist from the Way crew's tour of operations and were consulted (AIR/50/292) as well as the No. 103 Squadron ORB (AIR/27/816) between February and June 1944. A key source for Bill Way's story wished to remain anonymous but I thank him nonetheless for his work in bringing their lives to my attention.

Chapter Six

My sincere thanks and gratitude to Jack Trend for sharing his memories with me. What an emotive and remarkable journey to relive in detail! I am indebted to Mariska and Hans Van Dam for their local expertise in providing the evasion route taken by Jack across Holland and Belgium in map format. In addition, thanks to Albert Wheatley for allowing me to publish the photograph of the memorial unveiling in 2008. Finally, thanks to Martyn Ford-Jones (No. 15 Squadron historian) for casting his expert eyes over the finer details.

Chapter Seven

My thanks go to Geoff for his warm welcome and keen insight into his flying career, and to his daughter Carol Manduca for acting as the 'go-between' to overcome any technical issues with emails! I would steer anyone interested in learning more about No. 550 Squadron to visit the excellent 550squadronassociation.org.uk website run by Peter Coulter.

Chapter Eight

I would like to thank Terry and Jean, Fred's children, for their generous time and support in bringing their father's story together and providing copies of letters, photographs and the No. 460 Squadron bulletin, which I freely consulted, along with the No. 460 Squadron ORB and appendices. There is a 1999 work by John Watson that provides a full list of No. 460 Squadron pilots and crews that was also useful reference.

Chapter Nine

Firstly I would like to express my thanks to my cousin, Reg Joyce, for allowing me to carry out in-depth research into his RAF service, and for putting some meat on the bones of his extraordinary story. My appreciation extends to Jeff Boyling, the cousin of the pilot of LW143, for sourcing and providing the photographs. Additionally, I would like to thank my cousin, Ann Billington, for general assistance and for helping me fill in some of the gaps in Reg's story.

Chapter Ten

A sincere thank you to Chris Beare for her assistance with this chapter.

Chapter Eleven

My gratitude extends to Mr Oliver Clutton-Brock, Robert and Geraldine Connell (nephew-in-law and niece of Flight Lieutenant Jim Page), Warrant Officer Harold Brabin, RAAF (No. 102 Squadron Wireless Operator), Mrs. Maureen Pateman (daughter of Bob Brewer), Mrs Caroline King (grand-daughter of Bob Brewer), Mr Peter Willis (nephew of Fred Court), Mrs Elizabeth O'Keeffe (niece of Fred Court), Mr Doug Beecroft (writer and son of the late Flying Officer Jim Beecroft – No. 102 Squadron RAAF), and Sergeant Donald E. Leslie (No. 102 Squadron flight engineer).

INDEX